Table for One

Recreating a Life After Loss

LINDA C. DOMIS

Disclaimers

The book contains the ideas and opinions based on the personal experience of its author and is intended solely to provide helpful information.

It is offered with the understanding that neither the author, nor the publisher, are engaged in diagnosing or rendering any kind of mental heath treatment or any other kind of personal or professional services in the book. The reader should consult his or her own mental health or other competent professional before adopting any of the suggestions in the book.

The author and publisher specifically disclaim all responsibility for any liability, loss, or risk, personal or otherwise, that is incurred as a consequence (directly or indirectly) of the use and application of any of the contents of this book.

The names of people mentioned in the examples published within the book have been used with their permission or changed to protect their privacy.

Acknowledgments

Writing this book has been a painful journey and a labor of love. I would like to thank those individuals who pushed me to the finish line.

First and foremost, my writing coach, Dee Burks, who inspired me with her knowledge of the writing craft, her wit, her humor and her wisdom. Thanks for keeping me on track and accountable.

To Linda McLean, my friend and business coach for her mentorship and for recommending Dee. To my daily accountable partners (my Sassy Six) especially Orly Steinberg, who finished her first book as I was starting mine and showed me what was possible.

To Leslie McDonnell, my sounding board who listened to me endlessly for hours.

To Ginger Sorosky, my right arm and soul sister who helped me with the technical and clerical tasks when I wanted to throw my computer in the trash.

I am grateful for the many survivors of grief I interviewed who were so selfless in sharing their deepest feelings, fears and vulnerabilities in the hope of helping others. Your stories gave me the emotional energy to carry on when I wanted to quit, and helped me see the light at the end of the tunnel.

To my mother and grandmother who inspired me from the age of ten to be a writer. I know you are both smiling down from heaven and giving me a high five.

To my sons, Jeff and Ryan, who are both amazing men and brilliant writers. You make me want to be a better person every day. Thanks for always being my cheerleaders.

Dedication

To the love of my life, Timothy Alden Domis.
Gone too soon, but never forgotten.

Contents

Grief is the price we pay for love.

– Queen Elizabeth II

Chapter 1

When the World Stops Turning

I just went out for sandwiches!

For the longest time, I've thought about how I'd open this conversation about grief with you. That one sentence about the sandwiches has defined so many of my memories of my own journey through grief. It is exactly where I was and what I was doing when my world, as I'd known it, stopped turning.

I think it's a lot like how you remember exactly where you were and what you were doing when some big national tragedy happened. It's like that, only worse, because no one, and I mean NO ONE, can truly understand the trauma of your life changing in an instant. It was an instant, but an instant for me that ran in slow motion. I see it and feel it as vibrantly as I did in the moment and there are certain things that don't get fuzzy or dull no matter how much time has passed.

The moment of trauma and following events can't be absorbed or comprehended in real time for any of us. Your mind slows down and, though you are there watching the terrible happen, you aren't fully comprehending. Your mind can't catch up to the reality of what is, let alone process the implications. That is how it was for me.

I dearly loved my husband, Tim, and though you would think that goes without saying, I want to say it clear and loud for those in the back. I loved him deeply, but that love had nothing to do with the emotions that followed the trauma of his death. So first and foremost, I want you to set aside the guilt or hesitancy you might have as you think about the emotions that crash in on you when a loved one dies. Those emotions are inexplicable, difficult and defy our own ability to reason and that's okay. The feelings that come after have zero to do with how much you loved that person.

Death is traumatic even if its expected, but I didn't expect Tim to die. My husband had always been the picture of health. He'd never had a serious illness or issue. He was athletic, fit and so full of life that it wasn't even within my ability to imagine he would die suddenly.

We'd been married for decades and in that time, we'd built an incredible life together. As Realtors, we'd both been successful and together built a company that had over 250 employees. We were at the pinnacle of our careers, had a wonderful family, and a huge circle of friends. We both enjoyed working together and traveling, and by anyone's standards were living a wonderful life.

When Tim had a rather routine appointment due to a cough he couldn't quite shake, the last thing either one of us expected to hear was cancer. Honestly, I was in denial at first and so was he. He'd never even had a serious illness. But after some testing it was confirmed, and a relatively invasive surgery scheduled.

We both treated it as something he was going to go through, and we'd get through it. I'd be lying to say I didn't ponder the what ifs, but it seemed so incredulous to think he would really die, that I forced myself to focus on the positive. I did worry about what might happen if his recovery took longer than expected. But when I tried to talk to Tim about that, he just brushed it off. He insisted he'd be fine, and we'd talk about it later.

I wanted to believe him. I had to believe him to get through the long wait of the surgery. So, I was thrilled when he came through the surgery and things looked good. After only a few days, Tim was back home and feeling better. We were both relieved. Barely a week post-surgery, he was getting around and feeling so much better.

It was Sunday night and Sunday nights had always been our time. It was the one day we usually spent together at home. We'd cook a great meal, talk about the previous week or what was planned the next week. It was a time of real connection and I always looked forward to Sunday nights. That night we talked about cooking something, but he suggested getting his favorite sandwich from a place nearby that we both liked instead.

It was a great idea, I thought, and on the way out, I saw our little dog was begging for his dinner as he always did. I yelled back in the house that the dog was hungry and left.

Twenty minutes later, I came back in the house and found Tim lying in a pool of blood. Ice cold panic gripped me as I juggled the phone to call for help and tried to turn him over at the same time. My husband was well over six feet tall and muscular. I could not budge his body or do anything for him at that moment. Within minutes, the paramedics arrived as did our son, whom I also called.

I have to say that as we all arrived at the hospital, and the chaos of the next half hour swirled around me, I knew. I knew Tim was gone. The medical team was finally able to get a heartbeat, but it had been so long. I just stood in the emergency room and watched as raw emotion rolled over me. While I was dreading the inevitable, the most traumatic thing I had ever witnessed, before or since, was my grown son pulling up his dad's favorite song on his phone and holding that phone up to Tim's ear. Tears streamed down my son's face as he begged his dad to wake up.

My trauma was harsh and soul crushing, but watching my child also go through his own trauma, knowing the outcome was almost already certain, was devastating. Even now, the one image that may never lessen is seeing the pain on my child's face. My children loved their dad with everything in them and I couldn't stop that pain or make it better.

Barely an hour after I'd found Tim, his heart gave out and he died. It seemed like a lifetime I'd lived in just that one hour. Even now as I write this, the details are still so vivid and traumatic. I had friends who took me that night to their home, and I crashed. I cried hysterically, moaned to the universe for allowing this to happen, and questioned every step, every word, every move I'd made that day. It all came back to the same truth. Tim was gone.

By the middle of the next day, I was spent. My son had handled notifying most of the people who had to know, and I was grateful. Friends called and when I did pick up the phone, every conversation started with, "I just went out for sandwiches," and ended with me sobbing.

I think it's normal to second guess yourself and wonder if there was something, anything, you could have done. While doctors aren't always known for saying the best things when someone dies, there was one doctor who set my mind somewhat at ease. I had been beating myself up over the fact I was gone twenty minutes. Tim had fallen and bled quite a bit before I returned, and I felt responsible. As if I could have gotten him help faster, it would have mattered.

This doctor told me that Tim didn't die because he fell. He fell because he died. Those were simple words, but they meant a lot to me at the time and still do. He was letting me know that even if I'd been standing right there, I couldn't have stopped what happened or changed the outcome. Just that little gift of compassionate truth was enough to soothe some of my initial guilt, but the next few days were a blur.

Like many who deal with an unexpected death, I went through the motions of final arrangements, expressions of sympathy from family and friends as well as the actual funeral. I focused on getting through it all and I didn't really think beyond that.

One Death, Many Kinds of Grief

When someone dies, the whole family grieves, but everyone experiences it differently. The loss of a spouse is different than the loss of a parent. The loss of a child is different than the loss of a spouse. No two people have the same kind of grief, but often we expect everyone to deal with it in the same way, which is not even possible.

While I understand the necessity of allowing everyone to have closure, I have to say funerals are horribly traumatic for those who are suffering. Often the differences in grief process for each family member can produce hurt feelings and misunderstandings at the funeral. Not only had I locked my emotions away behind a stone wall just to get through the formality of the event, I also had to watch my children and grandchildren go through it.

My denial and avoidance kicked into high gear. All I wanted to do was go back to my life and carry on as if it hadn't happened. I wanted to grasp onto some semblance of normalcy having no idea that didn't even exist for me anymore. I wanted to block out all the terrible emotions and pretend.

Before I had this experience, I often wondered about people who lost a spouse and went right back to work. Why did they do that? Didn't they want more time? Didn't they have more 'grieving' to do?

Well, the answer to that for me was a resounding NO. NO, I didn't want more time to relive that trauma in my head every minute of the day I sat at home with nothing to do. NO, I didn't want more time to wallow in emotions that have no resolution. NO, I didn't want the judgement of other people who are talking about my grief and deciding if its 'good enough' or appropriate.

That clarity for me was the biggest reason I wanted to write this book. Grief isn't what we think it is or what we are told it is.

Grief is different for every single person yet the judgements of others, even close friends and family, can make it so much harder than it has to be.

> # Grief isn't what we think it is or what we are told it is.

We've been lead to believe there's a certain way grief is supposed to happen and a certain way that is appropriate to grieve. That is a huge disservice to every single one of us because grief never sticks to a plan or a bullet point list. Grief is messy. Grief is inconvenient. Grief never leaves.

At the time Tim died, I didn't understand any of this. I was just trying to survive. One thing I am so glad I did do was connect with a close girlfriend right after it happened who had lost a spouse a couple of months earlier. The one question I had for her was, "Will I survive this?" because honestly, I didn't know.

There was no clear path as to what to do, how to feel, or even if I was going to feel again. I was completely numb.

My girlfriend told me the truth and for that I will be forever grateful. She said, "Yes, you will survive, but it will not be easy. It may be the hardest thing you ever do." She was right.

For the first six or eight weeks I lived like a zombie. I tried to put one foot in front of the other and gain some sort of semblance of my life back, but it refused to fall into place. I was working, listing houses, doing the paperwork, and getting through each day only to come home exhausted and drained. I didn't eat regularly, I drank too much wine, and stared into the silent darkness for hours, my mind blank.

It was worse, I think, because Tim had such a big personality and since we worked together in our company, that absence was felt every second of every day. There was nowhere I could escape the weight of his loss. Many days I just wanted to magically shrug it off like a wet cloak; just pretend it hadn't happened. Fake it, in other words. Pretend to be happy and not think about it for a day.

I secretly enjoyed talking to new clients who'd never known Tim simply because we could discuss business and there wasn't that depth of sorrow in their eyes. I clung tightly to first one, and then a second girlfriend who had both lost a spouse and we became our own little support group. It was the one place where I didn't feel the need to talk about the trauma, or Tim, or tell the story for the thousandth time of how I just went to get the damn sandwiches.

I also had a cousin who had lost his wife and he was a brilliant shoulder to lean on when I got overwhelmed. In many ways, having that lifeline of people who understood and did not judge my grief, really saw me through some tough days. It's not that other people didn't sincerely want to help, they did. But what I realized was that some help actually makes you feel worse, not better.

For years I'd attended funerals of family or friends and offered my deepest sympathy. I'd said things like, "Oh, I'm so sorry for your loss. If you need anything I'm just a phone call away." I meant it, but those were worthless empty words.

I had no idea a grieving person might need to scream for a full five minutes and then sob for an hour while you listen and don't judge. I had no idea that a grieving person might want to talk about something, anything, other than the person they lost. In fact, I felt a little guilty at the times I'd brought up a deceased person thinking that might make the grieving spouse feel better or let them know I really cared. In my case, those things didn't help at all. Insead it forced me to relive the trauma all over again.

I think it's important to note that every person's grief is different and just because one widow or widower is comforted by something doesn't mean it won't have the opposite effect for someone else.

That is why there is no such thing as someone who 'knows what you are going through'. While some may have been through the death of a close loved one or even a spouse, their grief will be different than your grief. This is because we are all different people and each relationship we have is different.

This brings up the first big question we all ask about ourselves when we are grieving.

Am I Crazy?

Every single person who has gone through grief has, at some point, asked themselves if they are crazy. We all wonder if we are losing our minds as we react in ways we can't explain and don't understand. We all wonder if we are even doing this grief thing right as we feel the weight of other people's judgements. Either we are too sad or not sad enough.

> **My life as I had known it, did not exist anymore.**

Nothing it seems, is within our control anymore, least of all our emotions. We all feel as if our lives, even though not perfect before, are now completely off the rails.

I will say that I can look back on the person I was before my husband died and realize I was both naive and I think, entitled. I expected our lives to continue as they had for decades and why shouldn't they? We took care of ourselves, were successful, and had many people we loved and cared about. Nothing bad would happen to either one of us and, even if it did, the other could handle it, right?

But that's not how it works. It took me months to realize that my life as I had known it did not exist anymore. I tried to keep going, do the things I'd done before, and act as if I was fine. But nothing was the same. The void left by Tim in my life was like a huge sucking wound that never stopped. I couldn't escape his memory or his influence.

For months I pretended. I avoided being home at all on Sundays and when I was home alone, the chair where he'd sat every Sunday night loomed like a huge ghostly spectre in the room. The dream home we'd created felt like a large vacant dungeon and I did anything not to be there. On the Sunday nights when I couldn't escape, I found myself numbing the pain with wine, all the while wondering what was wrong with me. Surely other people handled this better, right?

I felt like my emotions were running me and as hard as I tried to tame them, they reared their ugly heads all the time. I snapped at people for no reason. Laughed hysterically at things that weren't that funny. Had the worst case of gallows humor that I couldn't shake for over a year. Said things to people that were completely out of character. To put it simply, I felt crazy.

After the initial shock of Tim's death, the lives of friends we'd known for years went back to normal, but mine didn't. Even when I tried to interact with friends, I felt awkward as if a part of me had been cut away and everyone stared at how damaged I was now. Tim and I were so much one entity at parties and events that I dreaded going to any at all.

It took a while for me to admit that my life as I'd lived it was gone. It had died with Tim and if I was going to move forward, I had to completely reinvent myself and my life. The whole idea of it was daunting. I had never really lived alone. I went from college roommates to married and stayed that way for decades. I didn't even know what my life was supposed to be, or even could be, as a single person over 50.

There comes a point where every person who has lost a long-time spouse especially, must leave the past behind and move forward. Not to forget, but to open your heart and mind to the future. You can't live in those memories every day, or your life will stagnate completely.

There is life after grief. A good life.

The most frustrating aspect of that realization is the fact that the people around you will fight you on it every step of the way. Many will see you moving forward as some kind of emotional betrayal, but it is not.

Humans have a huge capacity to love and loving another person doesn't mean you have forgotten about, or didn't love, the person that has passed. Grief allows you great potential for growth and understanding and part of that understanding is seeing that there is life after grief. A good life.

It is normal to feel crazy while you are grieving, I did. I longed for the past so much in those early months but hated any mention of it. It was as if every time I started to feel better, someone wanted to talk about Tim again and I was right back in the trauma.

The day after Tim died, I remember sitting up in the bed in

my friend's house. I thought about how everyone else got up this morning and went to work like any normal Monday. Their lives were the same as yesterday, and last week, and they were blissfully unaware anything bad might happen.

How could that be when my life had been so horribly and permanently altered? I never thought I would walk out of the house and never hear Tim's voice again. I never thought my last words to him would be about feeding the dog! I never thought I'd back out of the garage and my life would never be the same.

I just went to get some sandwiches.

It takes strength to make your way through grief, to grab hold of life and let it pull you forward.

– **Patti Davis**

Chapter 2

Nice People Don't Feel This Way

$\mathcal{W}$e all have heard there are five stages to grief. This knowledge of how we humans move through unexpected endings has been around since the late 1960s. Those stages are denial, anger, bargaining, depression and acceptance.

These stages of grief have become such common knowledge that we expect to go through them like steps in a self-help program. We convince ourselves that if we just follow the 'program', things will be normal again. We will be 'fixed', or cured, and our grief will be past.

I'm here to tell you that is not how it is. While I will talk more later in this book about the various stages you might experience after the loss of a loved one, I want to be clear that it is not easy or the same for every person. Some of these stages you might never experience, while others might linger for years.

However, because we expect our emotions to travel this assumed path of set stages, we can be taken completely by surprise when our grief refuses to follow that expectation. It is common for people not to experience all the emotions they have been told they are supposed to feel. It is also normal for one emotion in particular to overwhelm their life and dominate their emotions for years afterward.

For me, the dominate emotion was anger. Now I have always been an absolute professional as a realtor. I had to be in order to maintain and grow the business Tim and I had worked toward all those years. Because of that, I always, and I mean always, presented myself as a professional, which to me meant keeping my emotions under control.

While I am the type of person who privately gets angry when fearful, frustrated or discouraged, thankfully, there wasn't a lot of that in my life prior to Tim's death. However, afterward the anger in my life took me by surprise in many ways because I really didn't expect it. I like to believe that I am a nice person, and I was raised to be a nice person, but these emotions didn't fit into who I thought I was as a person or a professional.

Initially, I was angry because I felt Tim didn't take his situation or diagnosis as seriously as he should have. I know it's easy to say that now but even at the time, with him being so vital to our business and our life, he hadn't planned to die. We hadn't even really talked about death and here I was trying to deal with the fallout from his lack of planning. I was angry at being left behind and angry he didn't plan, which is completely normal for anyone in that situation.

However, that anger quickly grew over the next few weeks until it became an undercurrent of irritation with almost everyone and everything. I still presented myself as a professional to my clients and employees, but I felt impatient and annoyed with things that never even bothered me before.

Every time I had to deal with something that Tim left undone, I felt an irritation I couldn't really push aside, and it was that way with so many areas of my life. Often, when you lose a spouse, every emotion of abandonment you have ever felt in your life will come at you like a tsunami. This manifested for me as anger.

I was angry I felt like a stranger in my own home. I was even angry that other people were so nice to me when I didn't feel like I deserved their kindness. I felt so shattered and uncertain of who I even was and I felt very unworthy of anyone's kindness. Those emotions intensified my feelings of guilt.

When I was alone with my thoughts, anger rolled over me like giant waves and I seemed powerless to stop it, yet I forced myself to keep the emotion hidden from those around me. Unfortunately, trying to hide any emotion never works.

Anger is one of the primal emotions we feel when things are out of our control and nothing fits that definition more than death, especially a sudden or unexpected death. We have no control over death or the consequences it leaves behind. I had suddenly arrived in this world where everything was uncertain and unstable. I wanted answers but had none.

Other people wanted answers too, and they looked to me. My children, our employees, our friends. There were constant questions. Who was going to take over for Tim in the business? Would I sell the house? Was I going to keep working?

Questions upon questions and I wanted to provide answers. But they were answers I didn't have. I went through each day pretending I had a handle on things, and everything was going along fine. I had to be the strong one now, or so I thought.

It was as if the whole world was resting on my shoulders, and I didn't want it to. But I had to push through and hold it together not only for everyone else's sake, but for my own. I was afraid if I cracked even just a bit, I might lose control of my emotions completely. Still, all the unanswered questions buzzed through my head daily like a swarm of persistent gnats that refused to let me rest.

At night, invariably, I replayed the events in my mind. I was angry at the medical people who couldn't save Tim. I was angry at myself for not being there. I was angry at Tim. How dare he die! How dare he not plan for, or talk about, the possibility of him dying. How dare he leave me to pick up the pieces. How dare he leave so many things undone. Why was this so hard? What did I do to deserve this?

I wavered between trying to ignore Tim's death completely and being suffocated by the memories. My mental and emotional exhaustion was so complete I'd spend evenings staring at a blank television screen for hours having no idea how much time had passed.

Even though intellectually I knew the anger was misplaced, I still didn't understand why I was feeling that emotion above all others. How could I be angry at someone who died? It's not like that was his plan to die and ruin my life. I kept wondering, what is wrong with me? Nice people don't feel this way!

> # Everyone gets angry at death on some level.

Oh, but they do! They really do. I discovered that yes, everyone gets angry at death on some level, and it is very common for that anger to be focused on the person who died. The reason being that there is nowhere for that anger to go so the easiest target is the deceased. The issue is that 'nice people' often deny that emotion and try to pretend it doesn't exist. But anger will not be denied.

Anger manifests in numerous ways and can ooze into every aspect of who you are. Remember in the last chapter when I talked about feeling crazy? Almost every symptom I had, from random outbursts to gallows humor to crying or laughing at the wrong time were all due to the fact I was repressing my emotions, especially my anger. I felt guilty for having that emotion at all and even more guilty for being angry at Tim. I got it into my head that nice people didn't feel that much anger especially toward someone they love. But I did.

I realized later that much of my anger toward Tim was really anger at the fact I not only lost him, I lost the life we'd built together and shared. While I spent a lot of time grieving Tim's death, once I realized my life was never returning to what I'd known before, I had to grieve the loss of that old life as well.

The result was that I struggled to get through normal interactions and be nice to people when I'd never had that issue before. I was always great with people and loved interacting with clients and other professionals. Now I dreaded it in some ways. I had no choice but to go on so I did. I think forcing myself to keep going, saved me in so many ways.

For many professionals, and business owners, work can be the one bright light in a world of uncertainty after a loved one dies. It was for me. I needed the regular 'normalness' of a work routine and familiar actions. Listing homes, talking to clients, working with employees and other realtors, it was the most normal thing in my life and as difficult as it was at times, it gave me the push I needed to really work on myself. I didn't have the luxury to fall apart for months, weeks, or even days. There were people depending on me.

The truth is that even when we think we are hiding our emotions, we really aren't, as they will manifest even without our conscious knowledge. I got to the point that I felt like I couldn't trust my own emotions and tried so very hard not to feel anything at all sometimes.

Often it takes a while, and usually some outside perspective, to realize our personality has changed. Mine certainly had and I could feel it was off way before anyone actually brought it up. I had to get to the bottom of my own anger and find a way to deal with it as it was also starting to effect my health.

Why Am I So Angry?

As I previously mentioned, during grief most people experience what I refer to as a dominate emotion. Whether that is anger, depression or denial, the real issue is not the emotion itself. The real issue is that they must deal with the underlying cause. The first step for me was to stop denying my anger or pretend it didn't exist. It did. I was angry. I had to talk about all the reasons I was angry and what I was going to do about it. The stress from holding my anger at bay was causing headaches, indigestion and numerous other issues so it wasn't something I could continue to ignore.

I think it is also important to note that the whys behind your dominant emotion may not be something you discover immediately. It can take time to get to the bottom of the whys but you must take that time. There is no short cut and no, the emotions don't eventually go away. That was what I kept hoping. If I could pretend things were fine long enough for the anger to dissipate, I would be okay. But the anger didn't go away, in fact it got worse.

Those who have lost someone will often talk about that first year as if it wasn't really them who experienced it. Almost as if they were disconnected from it in a way. Your emotions are all over the place during those first few months. You haven't figured out anything and are focused on getting from one day to the next. I found that was definitely true for me. I held things together and from the outside, looked as if I was getting on with life.

I successfully braced myself for the first holiday season without Tim and got myself through the various family functions. It's interesting that those weren't real struggles for me because I could mentally prepare and box in my emotions to get through it.

The real struggle for me were the unexpected situations that appeared out of nowhere. The quick trip to the grocery store only to arrive home and realize I'd picked up items only Tim would eat. The exciting business deal where I absently picked up the phone and dialed his number to share it with him. The nights I jolted awake convinced I'd heard his voice.

Another widow I know describes these events as if you are strolling across a beautiful lawn, finally enjoying nature and feeling more like yourself, only to trip over a headstone. That is exactly what those unexpected events are like. You can't prepare in advance or brace your emotions and even though those events may be small, the emotions suddenly crash in on you again. Grief is a constant dance of two steps forward, one step back for months or years. It is not quick or easy.

Though every person's experience is different, most will recognize a similar pattern. Throughout this book I am going to talk about the reality of living with grief and that is an important point to understand. Grief is not something you really 'get over', it's something you learn to live with. The life you had, and your loved one's death, becomes part of you. The grief doesn't disappear.

I've grown increasingly irritated at the falsely happy self-help grief books that promote the idea of think happy, be happy. Life isn't like that and pretending, rather than understanding your emotions, isn't helpful for those in the midst of what is often the most difficult struggle of their life. While I'm a firm believer in getting to that good life again after a loved one passes, I also know you don't get there by pretending. I tried that; it didn't work. In fact, it made things so much worse.

An Alternate Reality

When I think back on what would have helped me most during that first year after Tim died, I go back to discussions I've had with girlfriends and other people I've met who have lost spouses. Almost all of them, me included, wished someone would have explained that you will live in an alternate reality for a while. For some its months, for others it can be a year or more. You will convince yourself things are fine, that you are fine, only to drop into deep sadness or depression unexpectedly.

One of the biggest struggles we have when trying to deal with loss, is our own expectation that things will be 'normal' at some point. It's like we keep doing the things we've always done hoping it will come back around to the life we knew. But it doesn't.

There is nothing more disconcerting than realizing you don't fit into your own life anymore. Everything is awkward and unfamiliar, even those tasks you've done a thousand times. I felt this intensely and much of my anger toward Tim had to do with the fact that I felt that I didn't fit into our life anymore. That had nothing to do with him and everything to do with me. Simple things like who will take out the trash were huge annoyances. When you have had a partner for decades, you fall into an expected way of being and when they are gone they leave a big hole; not only in your heart, but in your everyday life.

Few people realize that the moment a loved one such as a spouse dies, we become different people. Situations and relationships feel awkward and uncomfortable not because they have changed, but because we have changed. Our perspective has been tremendously altered and it's as if we are living a life parallel to that old life, but not really in that life anymore. While that may sound confusing, those experiencing grief will grasp it immediately. It's as if you are looking in on your old self and old life, but you can't cross that line to join in anymore.

When a spouse dies, we become different people.

This is frustrating, depressing and sad. In my case, it produced that overwhelming anger I was experiencing. I was looking for something to try or something that would work to 'fix' it. But there is no fixing your life when it has been so drastically altered. There is only moving forward, and you can't move forward while trying to get back to your previous life.

The other piece of alternate reality many of us struggle with during grief is the expectations of others. They read the same stages of grief article that we did, and they have their own expectations of how you should progress through those steps.

No matter what you do as you grieve you will, at some point (or many points in my case), feel the judgment from other people.

Some will voice their judgements outright, while others only whisper behind your back, but they all follow the same patterns. You are not sad enough, or you are too sad. You are getting out too soon, or not soon enough. You are too emotional, or not emotional enough. It seems no matter what you do or say it is scrutinized by others according to their expectations of how they think you should grieve.

The worst part is that close friends and family can be the most critical and it hurts. Their expectations place you in a no-win situation that you can't break free from because the judgement is everywhere.

You will overhear conversations of people you know making assumptions about you and your deceased loved one that have nothing to do with reality. For example, at the golf course where Tim and I spent a lot of time: "Oh, yesterday was Tim's birthday and you know Linda didn't seem upset at all. I think there were more problems in that marriage than they let on."

Really? There's anger again, my old friend. Am I supposed to prostrate myself out on the back nine crying my eyes out every year on Tim's birthday? Because if I did, I guarantee you my son would get a call about how I'd had a break down and should be committed.

No matter how you present yourself, people will infer things about your relationship that have nothing to do with anything. I really blame a lot of television cop shows for perpetuating this myth. How many times have you seen detectives watch the spouse of a deceased person and infer things about the relationship? While we all know that is fiction, people do that to you in real life, all the time.

Sell the house? She must be wanting to get rid of his memory. *Dare to be seen with a friend of the opposite sex?* She must have just married the last husband for money. *Actually laugh in the company of others?* Wow, she got past his death really quickly I bet those rumors of trouble in the marriage were right.

I realize some may read this and think this is in jest, but it is not. These are actual conversations you will hear and it can even come from those closest to you on occasion. Everyone has an opinion about your life and how you should lead it and they suddenly think that it's okay to share those opinions with you or anyone else that will listen.

I really struggled with this. Well-meaning people who started to tell me what I needed to do and how I needed to do it. I'll be honest, I wasn't exactly kind to those people and I'm not sorry. You have to do what is best for you in the moment and that means dealing with things as best you can no matter what others think.

The real issue I found with others' assessing your grief is that they absolutely refuse to allow you to change, even though you already have. Every step toward a different version of you they see as some kind of character flaw or failing, rather than a positive move forward. It's as if they are aghast that you dared change after someone died. Who do you think you are?

Reality is that your life, and how you live it, will never be the same and it takes some people, especially those who have known you for years, much longer to catch up to that idea. Some of them never do and it is quite common for many of your friends and acquaintances to become distant. There are people Tim and I spent a great deal of time with that I never see or talk to now. That is okay. Things have changed. I changed, and I had to accept the reality that not everyone will complete this journey with me.

The fact that our business was real estate also meant that there were unscrupulous competitors that tried to take advantage of Tim's death. They told clients our company was in shambles, and I was a mental case. You think it's ridiculous that anyone would believe that but when you are in a competitive industry, it can happen.

I was disgusted and determined to prove people wrong by working harder and being even more professional than ever. While the anger inside me roared at this kind of underhanded behavior there wasn't much I could do about it.

I find it interesting that as these changes and struggles happened in my life, that is when I missed my husband the most. I needed his humor, his wisdom, his counsel. He was my best friend for almost all of my adult life and that bond protected me in so many ways from the nasty things people would say or do. I needed to hear him laugh it off and tell me everything would be okay. But he couldn't and it wasn't.

I had to find my own way for the first time in my life and that was terrifying.

You never know how strong you are, until being strong is your only choice.

– Bob Marley

Chapter 3

Holding Pattern

One of the most unexpected aspects of grief for me was that first year. I like to refer to it as the holding pattern. It is a time when most people who are grieving are going through the motions of normal life while trying to adjust to the fact there is nothing normal about their life anymore.

It takes time and patience to figure out how to exist, let alone how to move forward and I spent much of that first year in a state of numbness. I think there are also some accepted grief reactions that are considered more 'normal' than others which only adds to the limbo you live in for that year.

In my case, I drank more wine, ate more cake and was desperate to not be alone. If you have a glass of wine before your husband dies, no one thinks anything of it. But after? Oh, the rumors go around you might become a lush. That type of quick judgement leads those in grief to hide almost everything they do which compounds the issues.

I felt like I had to hide to have a glass of wine and I did drink more as the allure of numbness is very strong when you are suppressing your emotions. I also gained some weight as I was stuffing my feelings by eating. I quickly learned that there is an assumption that losing weight after a loved one dies is somehow noble, but if you gain weight (even ten pounds) you have somehow let yourself go!

I also didn't want to be alone in the house, so I ate out with friends a lot which didn't help the drinking or the weight. Being home alone was when I most felt Tim's absence and I wanted to avoid feeling anything.

In many ways I was somewhat hypersensitive to peoples' judgements simply because I felt I had so many people watching me and expecting me to perform in a business sense. I think often during this initial phase of grief we are hardest on ourselves and that was certainly true in my case. We assume everyone else handles this better than we do and somehow we have to keep it together no matter what.

As a strong person, the last thing I was willing to admit was that I couldn't handle my emotions. However, there is so much turmoil after a death that no one can effectively handle it all no matter how much they pretend. There is work, family, and all the difficulties of figuring out how to recreate your life while having no idea what that even looks like.

Because everyone experiences grief differently and must deal with different circumstances, no one can tell you exactly how to handle it and inevitably we all have areas we don't navigate very well.

Comparison is a Thief

We all fall victim to the comparison game both in business and our everyday lives. Not only do we compare our experiences surrounding business success, parenthood, and marriage, we also compare our experience with loss. This is how we get the idea that everyone else does it better. Once you have lost someone, you will inevitably hear almost every friend or acquaintance tell you what their experience was like to lose their uncle, their grandad, or their dog (yes really). While some of these shared experiences are helpful, most are not. No one really knows exactly how you feel because they aren't you.

Comparing ourselves to others and feeling as if we come up short as we try to get through that first year can really be destructive, especially if the conversation is about how they got past their grief without any issues and now live this fabulous life. Know up front that's probably a lie anyway. We all have struggles as we travel through these unfamiliar emotions and if you spend too much time with those who aren't supporting you, it can stall your progress.

I found that I attracted people into my life that had somewhat similar experiences with the death of their spouse and because we could share our common struggles in a safe space, it was very helpful to me. I find that when the subject of grief comes up with a group of random people, often it can devolve into a series of tales as to who overcame the most. Like its some kind of horrible contest to be the most perfect. There seems to be a lot of people who desperately cling to the idea they must be perfect. As if to admit any weakness is some kind of failure.

> A lot of people desperately cling to the idea they must be perfect.

One of the interesting things I discovered about myself after Tim died is that I suddenly had an aversion to 'perfect' people. Those who were constantly striving to be better than everyone else or who wanted to present the idea they had every aspect of their lives under control.

They were constantly talking about others and measuring themselves against some invisible yardstick and while they had always done that, after Tim's death I had no tolerance for it anymore. It was as if they were seeking to deny the fact that we are all imperfect and we all suffer, especially with things like death. I felt my own inadequacies so strongly that having the idea of perfect in my face for any length of time was too much.

Thankfully the people that I naturally drew into my life were those like me; they were suffering but trying to do the best they could with their circumstances. Let me give you an example of one of those people.

I have a friend, Debbie, who I have known for almost 50 years. She also lost her husband, Dan, after a three-year battle with cancer. In that way, her experience was very different than mine, in that I lost Tim very quickly, but she had three long years of watching Dan decline. However, our struggles to cope during that first year after our husbands died drew us together.

When Dan died, he and Debbie had been married almost ten years. Dan was tall, handsome, and full of life. They had both been previously married and each had two grown children. Debbie's daughters, Ashley and Jessica, immediately developed a very close, strong bond with Dan. He had a great sense of humor and a wonderful positive presence when he walked into a room. The following is a summary of Debbie's own words describing what happened when Dan died and how she coped:

"Dan had a brutal and painful death after a three-year battle with cancer. I was his only caretaker, and the job of nursing him was overwhelming and exhausting. At the end, my big, strong husband was down to 90 pounds, and I was changing his diapers.

Dan was a kind man, but stubborn. When he got to the point he needed a hospital bed, he refused to have it put in the guest room. So, I had to have our bed disassembled to move the hospital bed into our master bedroom.

The last week of his life was the worst emotionally. I knew the end was near but so many people who we were close to us did not come to see me or help, as they "didn't want to see Dan so close to death." His adult children didn't even visit in his last months.

After he passed, I was overwhelmed with anger, grief and a loss of my identity. My whole life for three years had been taking care of Dan; ultrasounds, doctor appointments, chemo, radiation, and so many medical visits.

Once it was over, my thoughts turned to "now what?" I felt guilty because one of the biggest emotions I felt in that moment was RELIEF. Yes, relief. I was so ashamed of those feelings. I did not want Dan to die and did everything I could to help ease his pain, but it was mentally and physically exhausting. After three years, I was glad he wasn't in pain anymore, but my own emotions punished me for being relieved from the grueling life of a caretaker.

Once Dan passed, there were so many more emotions that bubbled to the surface. Dan had told me that everything was taken care of prior to his death and that I shouldn't worry. I soon found out it wasn't.

I couldn't access our bank accounts for two weeks until I had his death certificate because it was a Joint account. The cable company shut off our cable and I couldn't get it back on because it had been in Dan's name. I spent hours on the phone with credit card companies, utility companies, and so many others explaining his death and trying to figure out how to keep everything going.

Planning Dan's funeral was also an unexpected nightmare. Dan's grown children and ex-wife, who were nowhere to be found when he was dying, now wanted to force their opinions on his services. They criticized and second guessed every decision I made, and it increased my stress tremendously. I did my best to be cooperative and stoic, knowing how we are all effected differently when someone dies but it was a very difficult time. I set my own grief aside to comfort them, as well as my daughters and grandchildren who had lost their "Papa."

Trying to adjust to my new normal was even more difficult. My life hadn't been any semblance of normal for over three years, what was it supposed to be now? People in general don't know what to say when you lose a spouse, so often they don't say anything, and you are left with painful awkwardness.

I'm rather shy by nature, and I was happy to go out with some of our couple friends, but I felt like a 5th wheel in a group of all couples. As a result, I became increasingly lonely, depressed, and isolated.

I knew I needed to deal with the grief, so I tried a support group recommended by the hospice department that had helped with Dan. The first group I attended was led by a woman and there were all women in the group. I was surprised to discover that some of the women had been meeting for over five years and had never even removed their husbands clothing from the closet. Again, I knew grief was a process, but I also knew this group was not for me. The group leader seemed to be enabling the women to stay stuck in a state of fear.

Yes, fear. Because dealing with grief means dealing with your fear. The fear that you will change, that you will feel those horrific feelings, the fear of facing your own mortality. Even the fear of living again and dealing with the guilt that you may go on and thrive without the love of your life by your side. I knew I wanted to live.

During that last week of Dan's life, I searched for something to hold on to. I found this quote, "You have to keep living until you are alive again." I made that quote my mantra.

I found a different group called Grief Share, and it was a life saver. I went to a special seminar right before the holidays on how to get thru those difficult weeks. It was wonderful. Slowly but surely, I started to feel alive again.

Three years later, life is so much better. I am dating a wonderful man, I have another beautiful granddaughter, and I'm competing again as an equestrian (not bad for being almost 70)! I still miss Dan terribly, but I'm a survivor, a thriver and I know now I can get through anything."

I love Debbie's story because she has overcome so much and has come out the other side with a great life. One of the first things I asked my widow friends when Tim died was, Will I survive this? Both mine and Debbie's stories are proof that you can and will survive but how you choose to get through that pain is up to you.

Don't Fear the Reaper

There are several areas of Debbie's experience, and my own, that I want to take a deep dive into and the first of those is fear. We all fear death to a certain extent, but I have come to understand that fear is a great liar. Death is nothing to fear, but change, that is what we all really fear. When we fear the idea of someone dying, we are really fearing the idea of how we will live without them.

For those of us who lose a spouse, the future is the big unknown. While you are immediately caught up in the trauma of the death, the funeral and things that must be done, what you really fear is the unknown that lies beyond. That is what makes that first year so very hard as you try to figure out a path through unfamiliar territory.

We are caught up in a whirlwind of change and every single thing in our life changes after a death. There is a giant hole in every aspect of what you thought life would, or could, be. I imagined that I'd grow old with Tim, we'd eventually retire and ride off into the sunset, but that didn't happen. Every single part of my being from how I started my day, to who made breakfast, and who took out the trash was altered.

I have to admit those first weeks and months its very much like living in a haunted house. You can almost see, smell and touch them as if they are still there. Its as if they stepped out for a minute and will be right back. It takes time to allow the idea to sink in that it will never be.

Those first weeks and months, its like living in a haunted house.

I didn't have it in me to make a lot of changes to the house because I really didn't think it would matter. Everything about that house, our dream house, was wrapped up in Tim and it made me so sad. The one place I wasn't sad was the beach house and so I began renovating it with the help of a friend. I wanted a space that was completely me where I wasn't reminded of Tim's loss constantly.

I asked my friends what they did first after their spouses died. One got rid of all the furniture, another only got rid of the bed. Still another never set foot in the house again and sold it.

We each have our own ways of dealing with that lingering sadness and that is a first step for most people. But we all continue to carry fear. Fear we will have a breakdown, fear we are crazy, fear there will never be any real normal in our lives ever again.

One of the most important things I learned about fear is that you must take action. Fear has a way of stopping you in your tracks. It stalls your progress and your plans. We easily slip back into the inertia of existing rather than moving forward. I found this to be true several times that first year. Things would improve a bit and seem to be on track, then I'd hit a period where I felt lost, awkward and unsure of myself again. It was a back and forth, up and down for months all the while I kept my emotions under a tight lid.

Many of our actions and reactions don't make sense in the moment. It is only when we look back that we understand what we were going through. That is how I see it now. I was so fearful of being discovered. Of people finding out I wasn't handling things as well as other people seemed to. Of needing help to move forward.

I remember going to a real estate conference about six months after Tim died. I didn't really want to go but we had some new people in our office that were attending and I felt like it was my responsibility to be there so I went. Many of the colleagues in attendance were people I knew from all over the country and most I had not seen since Tim died. Of course, they all knew Tim as we'd been such a strong team at those conferences. But this time it was like reliving the awkwardness of the funeral all over again.

I remember sitting in a seminar and suddenly I just couldn't anymore. I got up and left. I walked down the corridor and the only thought on my mind was I had to get away. I felt crushed by the sadness again and it was overwhelming.

As I walked down the hallway, coming the other direction were two men that I know very well. One, Brad, had also lost his wife a couple years earlier and as they came down the hall, we locked eyes and I knew he knew. There is something about those of us who have been through grief that allows you to immediately spot someone who is at the end of their rope. Brad spotted my distress though I thought I was hiding it.

We spoke for a few minutes about what was going on with me. He calmed my fears and reassured me we all travel this same road of uncertainty thinking we are crazy. I asked if that sadness would ever go away or not catch me off guard at some point. He was honest and said no. But he did give me the understanding that fearing the emotions or sadness was not allowing me to move forward.

Once I got home, I immediately called a therapist that specialized in grief. That was the real beginning of my healing as I let go of that fear. Fear of what others would think, fear of my own emotions, fear I might not get through it. That was my path but it was almost a year in the making and that is a truth most people discover: it takes time.

The real point and joy of stories like Debbie's and my own, is that there is a way through. It's not easy and its not a quick fix, but you can heal your heart and find joy again.

Throughout the rest of this book, I'm going to talk about the stages of grief I, and others, have experienced. I want you to see how very different we all are so that you will realize there is no one way to grieve. I want you to understand that we all struggle. We are all afraid. We all have setbacks. But those don't have to define us.

I decided toward the end of that first year that I would not be defined by Tim's death. He would have wanted me to go on without him. To grow and become the best version of myself. We each deserve to give that gift of release to ourselves after the loss of a loved one. Only by embracing change, and setting aside our fears, can we reinvent our lives to once again find joy and happiness in whatever form we choose.

Grief is not a disorder, a disease, or a sign of weakness. The only cure for grief is to grieve.

– **Earl Grollman**

Chapter 4

Grief is not Linear

*G*rief is one of the most difficult things any human will experience, and we may go through many different types of grief throughout our lives. People grieve when they go through a difficult breakup or divorce. You may grieve if you lose a job or had a friendship end. Then of course, there is death of a loved one whether that is a parent, partner or a child. Not only do we grieve the loss of someone dear, we can even grieve our own mortality if we receive a terminal diagnosis.

Because grief is so difficult, it has been studied extensively by mental health professionals for decades. A Swiss psychiatrist, Kubler-Ross first introduced her five-stage grief model in her book *On Death and Dying* in 1969. This model was based on patients she worked with who were terminally ill and Kübler-Ross listed the stages of grief as Denial, Anger, Bargaining, Depression, and Acceptance.

Kubler-Ross Grief Cycle

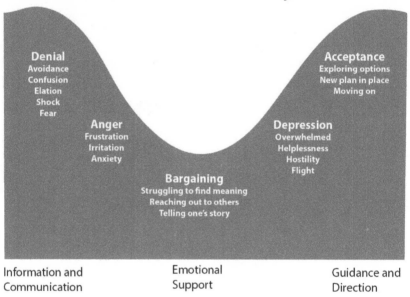

Denial
Avoidance
Confusion
Elation
Shock
Fear

Acceptance
Exploring options
New plan in place
Moving on

Anger
Frustration
Irritation
Anxiety

Depression
Overwhelmed
Helplessness
Hostility
Flight

Bargaining
Struggling to find meaning
Reaching out to others
Telling one's story

Information and
Communication

Emotional
Support

Guidance and
Direction

While these stages of grief are widely accepted now, her model originally stirred up some controversy among professionals because many of them made the same assumption that many of us still do, that those who grieve go through these stages in order and fully experience all of them.

Of course, that is not true, and was not what her model was saying at all in my opinion. These five stages are just the ones people commonly experience. However, some people never experience all the stages while others get 'stuck' on a specific stage for an extended period of time. The bottom line that we all should understand now, is that grief is not linear. We don't travel the stages like stairs on a staircase finishing one before going onto the next. In fact, we can experience several stages at once.

I am not a clinical professional at all, but I can tell you what it was like to go through some of these stages and how it affected me. The closest analogy I can come up for what my grief was like is to say it was somewhat like a potluck, meaning I never knew what I would experience. It depended on the day and the circumstances as well as my own mental state at the time.

It is easier to look back and identify what stage of grief I was in at certain times than it was to recognize them as they were happening. I, like so many others, wafted in and out of emotions, back and forth between these stages of grief for a long time and you probably will too. Healing is not a straight trajectory, nor is the path clear of how you get from loss to a new life.

I will say that the grief potluck was at its worst during those times I was exhausted, drained, tired beyond belief or not feeling well. I'd like to tell you to take care of yourself from the outset in order to avoid much of these down times, but that wouldn't be fair. While I'd always taken care of myself, my health took a huge backset during those first few months of grief.

I was finding comfort anywhere I could – a bottle of wine, a slice of cake, calorie packed pasta – anything that would distract me from feeling. You will probably do some of the same and there is no shame or guilt in trying to cope. But taking care of your physical health will help everything in those first months.

I'll also remind you that grief never goes away. It's not like you get through the stages of grief this week and are 'fixed' by Friday. You can't check off the stages like a to-do list. While there will be a dramatic improvement after a couple of years, the stages can, and often will, return in some form for years and usually when you least expect it. When things are going well or you have that next grandchild, or achieve some goal, those are the times the sadness will creep back in. Just being aware of this fact, and expecting it, will lessen the effects when it happens.

Now I want to take each stage of grief and talk about it separately. The ones I experienced, I will share my experiences with you. The ones I didn't, I'll share from some of the friends I've come to know who did experience them. I think reading those experiences and understanding the emotions we felt will help you connect to your own grief in a real and deep way.

Denial

I don't know how I got it into my head to think that the denial part of grief meant that someone refused to believe their loved one died. Because of that, I thought for the longest time that I completely skipped this denial thing. But that is not the full definition. Sure, there are those that want to believe there's been a mistake or perhaps their loved one isn't really dead, and that is definitely denial.

However, denial has a second, and much larger, definition in reference to grief. Denial also means denial of your emotions. This is the denial I experienced and the same one many other people experience too. I think a much better definition of this stage of grief would be the 'I'm fine' stage. It's when you completely block your feelings and pretend everything is fine. You are fine, work is fine, family is fine , everything is FINE!

I can't even tell you how many times I said the words 'I'm fine' those first few months. I said it at the funeral, at the office, every time anyone asked how I was it was always 'I'm fine' when I knew I was not fine.

I didn't want to talk about it, hear about it, or even think about it.

Part of this stage for me was the fact that I didn't want to rehash Tim's death repeatedly. I didn't want to talk about it, hear about it, or even think about it.

Denial is one of the first coping mechanisms that kick in when we experience any kind of trauma and with good reason. The emotions that result from a death would overwhelm each one of us if we didn't have the ability to compartmentalize those feelings. We lock them away and do our best to motor though the difficulty of getting through the trauma and on with life. Even though we are putting off dealing with the horrible emotions, by allowing our minds to slowly work though the trauma over time, it spares us from breaking down completely.

My denial lasted for months and part of that was I felt I had to be strong for those around me. It's as if I felt giving into those awful emotions would damage me or damage them.

There was also that idea that I didn't want to dump a bunch of emotional baggage onto other people.

When someone asks how I am, I am not the type to share my innermost thoughts. I always give a positive 'happy' response. Part of that is habit and I didn't want to be viewed any differently. I didn't want to be the downer in a crowd of friends or family so I put on a happy face. Of course, that didn't last because eventually we all must deal with our emotions if we are ever to move forward.

Anger

I have already talked about the anger I felt after Tim died. I experienced this stage almost from the beginning and still do on occasion. Anger can present in various ways when you are grieving especially with a traumatic or unexpected death. You want to raise a fist to the universe at the unfairness of it all! It is common to take out your anger on family, friends and even yourself. However, anger can also manifest as anxiety.

Anxiety is a fear of the future but it can have devasting effects on your emotions. When I got anxious, I would run things constantly through my mind and worry over every little decision. I'd lay awake and thoughts would race through my mind such as,

"Would Tim have made that decision?"

"What would Tim do?"

"How long can I keep going when I'm exhausted?"

"Who will take care of things if I fall apart?"

"Would Tim be okay with this?"

In my case, anger/anxiety was also part of my denial. I felt a lot of guilt for being angry at all and had constant anxiety over decisions. I hated that uncertainty and couldn't seem to trust my own judgement. I had always been so sure of myself, and it made me feel weak in a way I did not like or want to accept.

Bargaining

The bargaining stage for me showed itself as I tried to hold my life together. I would constantly tell myself that if I could get past this one event or issue, everything would be okay. If I could get through this week, this month, or this year these horrible emotions would go away. At least that's what I hoped.

Bargaining is a problematic stage of grief for many. The reason is that we are often bargaining with ourselves, God or the universe to get back to our 'normal' life. But that life doesn't exist anymore. We just haven't fully realized it yet. So we keep the same habits, go through the motions of the life we used to live trying to force things back into the normalcy that was familiar.

Bargaining, like the other stages we are discussing, seldom exists in a vacuum. We don't experience that stage in isolation. It is combined and compounded by the other stages of grief until it feels as if you are being suffocated by them. Let me explain how that worked in my life. I would frequently experience the first three stages of grief on the list all at the same time and it went something like this:

I'd put on my positive, professional face and set aside my emotions (all of them) to get through the day. I already talked about how an undercurrent of irritation and anger was my near constant companion and I worked to keep that irritation under wraps and hidden which was exhausting. It was so exhausting that there were many days I'd secretly whisper, *just let me get through this last meeting and keep it together until I get home.*

Just let me keep it together until I get home.

I was bargaining with myself while trying to manage my anger and pretend everything was fine. This is what was so mentally and emotionally draining. It was all I could do to manage until I got home and didn't have to pretend anymore.

One of the worst parts of this type of emotional juggling is that your exhaustion compounds on itself. I had a lot of internal anxiety about the future and what was going to happen, and that anxiety would cause me to lose sleep. There were times I barely slept at all and yet I'd go into work the next day and pretend, once again, that I was fine.

The stages of denial, anger and bargaining were most of my experience especially that first year. They intensified as I started to understand my life would never, ever be the same.

Depression

One of the stages I didn't experience a lot of after Tim's death was depression. Usually, when someone who is grieving gets depressed, they tend to withdraw and isolate.

I was the opposite in that I actively sought out people so I wouldn't be alone. However, depression can be a huge stage of grief for a lot of people.

While grief is a normal part of life, it can become severe in some cases. Approximately 10-15% of people will have severe reactions to grief which can lead to depressive episodes. This is especially true if they struggled with depression prior to their loved one's death.[1]

Often those who experience depression will feel overwhelmed and helpless to the point they refuse to get out of bed and can't really function.

Depression is also one of the more accepted forms of grieving because it is such an obvious association to be very sad when a loved one dies. It's almost expected that you experience depression at some point.

I will say that I struggled with depression at other times in my life, notably during postpartum and menopause. So I understand how debilitating it can be. I have always been open about that struggle and did not hesitate to seek help, as depression can be so overwhelming.

While there were certainly down times after Tim's death, I would describe those episodes as more melancholy. I never got to any sort of clinical depression at that time, but other people often do when they are dealing with grief.

For some people, grief can present itself as very similar to post traumatic stress. They may exhibit addictive tendencies, risky behavior, suicidal thoughts and struggle

1   Bonanno, George A. (2004). "Loss, Trauma, and Human Resilience: Have We Under-estimated the Human Capacity to Thrive After Extremely Aversive Events?". American Psychologist 59 (1): 20–8. doi:10.1037/0003-066X.59.1.20. PMID 14736317.

with overall mental health.[2] This is especially true for individuals over 65 who have lost a spouse after decades together.

I met Janie not long ago and learned her story. Depression can come from many issues after the loss of a loved one, but when you have small children, as Janie did, the pressure to set aside and ignore those feelings is high.

Janie saw her life pass before her eyes the day she lost her husband Derek. At only 43 years old and with 4 children under the age of 11, Janie was not prepared for the reality of widowhood. Darling Derek, the love of her life, was diagnosed with a rare form of blood cancer that took his life in less than 3 months. He was only 45 years old. Because of a recent job change, Derek had not enrolled in a private life insurance plan, and Janie and the children were left practically penniless with his passing.

"It's so lonely, and so so hard. I try to be Mom and Dad now to the girls and Jacob, but I constantly feel I'm failing them. They are such great kids, and they didn't deserve to lose their "daddy" so young. I'm afraid our youngest, Katie, who was only 2 when he died, will never remember him. I've always been a good Christian, but I found it hard not to be angry at God for taking him away from me. I know intellectually that's not the case, but my broken heart has a mind of its own, and I'm struggling."

The sadness was prolonged and overwhelming as Janie sank deeper into her grief. When a friend recommended a therapist that specialized in grief therapy, Janie found an inner strength and wisdom that began to lift her depression

2   Rosenzweig, Md; Prigerson, Phd; Miller, Md; Reynolds Iii, Md (1997). "BEREAVE-MENT AND LATE-LIFE DEPRESSION: Grief and Its Complications in the Elderly". Annual Review of Medicine 48: 421–8. doi:10.1146/annurev.med.48.1.421. PMID 9046973.

and despair. She found her way back to a new church where she could make a fresh start as her own person, not "Derek's widow." Her church connections led to a well-paying part-time job with flexible hours so she could be home for the kids after school.

Three years after Derek's death, Janie is beginning to thrive again. She's even dating Connor, a single father of three, she met in a bible study for single parents. Janie has also taken classes in grief therapy, so she can help others who have struggles with widowhood. "I'll never be over what happened to Derek," she remarks, "but I'm beginning to feel joy and love again, and the new church and therapy helped me find my way back to the Lord. It's still very hard, but the kids are doing well in school and their inner strength amazes me. I feel Derek is really helping watch over us from heaven."

Depression during grief, while common, is difficult at best. The overwhelm of trying to start a new life along with the demands of parenting and all her financial stress, could have forced Janie into an unrecoverable downward spiral. That didn't happen because she chose to get help. That is a key decision that can't be understated. Grief is so devastating that I am often amazed any of us get through it without imploding.

Acceptance

Though this stage of grief is listed last, in my experience, the sooner you can reach acceptance the sooner you can start to heal. With this stage, like with denial, there is some confusion about what it means. Acceptance, in this context, means that you have realized you can never get back to your old life and in order to move forward, you must embrace change. It is really not about the loss of your loved one per se, it is about you and how you plan to live going forward.

I reached acceptance within that first year but no matter when it happens, acceptance is really the beginning, not the end. I had to accept that I must recreate my entire life and that was scary. I had to let go of the life I once had and stop trying to get back to the old normal. My way forward was to create a new normal and see where it led.

It was uncertain and unknown but also very freeing. As you go through your own grief you will probably discover, as I did, that you become very uncomfortable with the way things are. It is as if that old life and those old habits now feel like a suit that has grown too small. It is confining and awkward. That is your first clue that you are growing and changing.

I started my own journey of acceptance by making a couple of decisions. The first one was that I was not going to let myself be defined by Tim's death. Up to that point it was as if he was the ghost in the room. Always there, but not there.

Every part of our business, our home and our lives together were infused with his presence. His death became a defining watershed point for months. It seemed as if every conversation was about either 'before' or 'after' Tim's death.

I had to reframe my thoughts from before and after, to this is my life now. It is not mine and Tim's life, it's just me and I must create a life that is uniquely mine.

The second decision I made was that I wanted to live. I didn't want to merely exist in this limbo between the old and new. I wanted to get to that place of healing and have a good life again even if I had no idea what that life might look like. I was determined that my best days were ahead of me.

I have seen people who are grieving who reject this idea of acceptance as if it's the ultimate betrayal of their loved one. As if wallowing in their grief for years will somehow prove they really loved them. This is unfortunately more common than you might think with those who lose a spouse and refuse to reengage with life. Staying in that grief stage is like a comfort zone they refuse to move on from.

> ### You must move on to get to a good life again.

Again, as with every stage of grief I'm not implying that it is easy. Starting over is so very hard for many of us, but you realize you don't have a choice and you must move on if you are going to get to a good life again.

Along with the many widows I talk to, I also encounter quite a few widowers. Because so many men tend to be rather stoic and not show a lot of emotion, sometimes their loneliness is compounded because the grief isn't acknowledged as easily or in the same way.

Everett is that kind of person, rather stoic and private, so his story was really poignant to me:

"It's been almost 20 years and it still feels like yesterday"

Everett and Ruthanne were married for 22 years, happy with three children when Ruthanne was diagnosed with ovarian cancer. In 1989 this was a death sentence, but Ruthanne rallied and battled the disease bravely for 14 years. Except for the last three months of her life, she had great quality of life. They traveled the world, were fulfilled with loving grandchildren, and had a vast, active circle of friends. Ruthanne had that "Princess Di quality". She walked into a room and lit it up like a Christmas tree. She was beautiful, smart and the world's best listener. Everybody loved her.

When she died in 2003, the family was in shock. Even though the end was coming, no one really accepted it, because Ruthie had cheated death for so long. Her grown children, Kristin, Everett and Amanda, were not prepared for the light to go out so quickly. Ruthanne died six days before her 56th birthday. Her family, friends and business colleagues were devastated.

Everett had spent the last 14 years managing his life around Ruthanne's various treatments, doctors' appointments, and surgeries. He had been a well-paid salesman in the catalog printing industry, but the rise of the internet and digital marketing was slowing making his job obsolete.

After the loss of his wife, Everett found himself widowed and out of a job. He writes, "Much of our savings was depleted because I wanted to spend as much time with Ruthanne as I could living life while she was healthy enough to do it. To this day I don't regret it, even though I've had to pay the price."

At first, Everett and Ruthanne's circle of "couples' friends" included him in their dinners and get-togethers. It worked out okay until he started dating after several months of being alone. He tried bringing his new dates around to meet his friends, but it became clear very quickly that any substitution for Ruthanne would not be accepted. His friends basically dumped him.

Everett turned 60 that year and found himself with no job, no wife and very few friends. "Men are not supposed to cry or show any weakness," remembers Everett, "but basically I still came home every night and cried." My whole life had been working and taking care of Ruthanne. In six months' time, my entire life fell apart."

But Everett's a survivor. He answered an ad in the newspaper and became a school bus driver. He found a new circle of friends at the bus company and a passion for what he did. "I interacted with a lot of young people driving the bus and came to realize I could be a positive force in their lives." He adopted a dog which made the nights at home less lonely.

Slowly, Everett put his life back together and has found new love with Leslie, a woman he met at the bus company. "There's not a day that I don't miss Ruthanne, but I know she would want me to be happy. Life is short and precious, and I intend to keep living It to the fullest."

Signs and Symptoms

As I said at the beginning of this chapter, you may or may not experience all the stages of grief, but you will experience some and along with those will come some physical signs and symptoms that you will want to watch out for. Some people like to think our bodies and minds operate in different areas, but I can tell you for certain that they are interconnected especially during grief.

Physical symptoms manifest quickly when your mind and spirit are troubled. Some of these can be obvious, others quite subtle; but all build on one another adding to your stress and anxiety.

The first obvious sign for me was crying to the point of exhaustion. Once the shock waned, I experienced frequent headaches as I tried to 'keep it together'. I also had tremendous difficulty sleeping and this was an issue on and off for the entire first year! There were days and weeks on end I woke up with a stiff neck and shoulders. My jaw hurt from grinding my teeth in my sleep or clenching them unconsciously.

You will probably question just about everything.

My appetite changed and while I wasn't eating a lot more, I was eating comfort food. Other people lose their appetite completely and not only lose weight but also have very low energy.

On a deeper level I think you can easily go down the rabbit hole mentally as you question your purpose in life or question your faith. In fact, you will probably question just about everything, I know I did.

I read that one of the symptoms of grief is feeling detached from your life or isolated. I can only describe this as feeling as if you are a spectator to your own life where you watch what is happening but don't have any emotional attachment to it. It's a very odd feeling.

Once you have lived with grief for a few months, the anxiety and worry (stress) can lead to extreme fatigue as well as aches and pains. You feel awful on top of having to deal with starting a new life. It is as if it slowly drains your life force and its all you can do to put one foot in front of the other.

Like with the stages of grief, you may experience all these signs and symptoms or only a few. However, how you feel and how you deal with these issues is critical to your future.

I caution people to get help sooner rather than later and to not let these physical issues slide. They don't go away and over time will only get worse. While I understand how difficult it is to focus on anything, it is critical for those in grief to eat well (as best they can) and get at least a little exercise. Your emotions will reach an equilibrium over time but if you've allowed those emotions to negatively impact your health, you will still have a long road to travel.

Our grief is as individual as our lives.

— Dr. Elisabeth Kubler-Ross

Chapter 5

You're Doing it Wrong

To say that navigating the grieving process is a mine field of emotions is a huge understatement. I think as humans we all try to fit things into a nice neat little box. A box we can define, label, and control to a certain extent. Grief is not like that, at all, but we want it to be.

We want a shortcut to quickly get past the pain in whatever form we experience it. However, there is no shortcut and what helps one person may not help you.

This is one of the reasons that though I listed the stages of grief in the last chapter, I don't intend for people to take them as absolutes. Every person and every grief is different. There are times when you grieve a close loved one and the grief follows an expected and relatively mild transition through various stages – if you even experience some of the stages at all. Then there are times someone passes, maybe not even someone that was extremely close to you, and yet you find it devastating. This has more to do with who you are, and what you are dealing with at that moment, than it does the person who passed.

Grief has its effects depending on where we are in our own lives and what affects us at the time. We are all moving through this life the best we can and depending on our own growth and relationship to the deceased, our grief will be different. I've had those who have had more than one spouse pass, talk about those differences in grief and how profound they are, and it's not limited to the loss of human loved ones either.

For some, the passage of their pets can affect them more traumatically than the passing of humans that are family. It's not unusual for this fact to produce extreme guilt and shame for someone because they think people 'should' be more important and thus grieved more deeply.

However, for many pet owners, the special bond they have with their animal is much harder to get past. I will say there is no judgement from me for that. Everyone's grief, whatever the root cause of that grief, is unique and no one can tell you how you should feel or how that grief should manifest itself.

Guilt and Shame

The idea that we are somehow doing grief wrong can produce intense feelings of guilt and shame. It's as if we feel we must conform to an expected way of grieving and if we step out of what is deemed normal or acceptable, there's something wrong with us. All I can say is that I think every single person who has ever grieved for anything has had at least a brush with these emotions. Almost all of us have looked in a mirror at some point along the way and wondered, "Am I doing this wrong?"

The issue from my perspective is that box we keep trying to fit grief into. Grief produces so many emotions that are difficult and uncomfortable, that people would rather hide those emotions or push them into the background to appear 'fine'. It is easier to fake it and appear as if life is going on as expected than it is to talk about those emotions and work through them. But in the end, we all must work through them one way or another.

I felt the emotions of guilt and shame on occasion as so many people in grief do. Sometimes it was in response to something someone said that made me feel as if my grief wasn't right or not good enough. Other times it was in response to my own thoughts that I didn't understand or that didn't seem logical. I experienced a lot of frustration with others who insisted I grieve a certain way or a certain length of time. I felt as if I wasn't being allowed to get through it and my grief seemed to be a constant two steps forward and one back.

It doesn't take long for anyone who is constantly confronted with these emotions and opinions from others to start to doubt themselves. For me, this had the effect of making me even more determined to carry on and repress those uncomfortable feelings. I became hypervigilant that no one see me 'break down' or somehow perceive that I was struggling with grief. That culminated in the idea that I was completely doing this grief thing wrong and that got worse as more time passed.

I felt I couldn't win no matter what path I chose.

There is a specific point when those who grieve will really feel the effect of all these negative emotions and that is usually when they start to feel they are ready to move on with their life. It is at that time there will often be more comments or much harsher judgement from friends or family and that judgement will once again make you question yourself. I know I did.

I wondered if, as some suggested, that my willingness to move on was covering up the grieving I still needed to do. I think this is especially true when you move on to a new relationship. Some people in your life will see that as good no matter when it happens. Others will see it as too soon or disrespectful to the one you lost no matter when it happens. I felt I couldn't win no matter what path I chose.

The truth is that you will never please anyone else and you can't experience your grief, and get through it, by waiting on a consensus from others as to how you should live your life. This is one area in which I really valued the community of individuals that I gathered around me who were also experiencing grief. It was in that safe space that we could discuss the feelings of shame and guilt as we all tried to both live our lives and move forward.

This is also an area where I appreciated getting my own therapist. I think getting an outside, and professional, opinion on how you are dealing with your grief can be invaluable. I stress professional here because so many people will go to counselors or advisors who are not grief therapists, and these non-professionals can do a significant amount of damage.

When we are in a raw and vulnerable emotional state, comments or judgements made by those we view as an authority, even if they are not grief professionals, can have a tremendous effect. Individuals not specifically trained in grief often merely relate their own experiences or viewpoints no matter what you really want or need.

This is frequently where people get the idea they are doing it wrong. They hear they must go through the expected stages of grief in a certain order and if they don't, then they are not dealing with reality. As you can imagine, if you are told repeatedly you aren't dealing with reality, when you know you are, it can cause lasting damage.

Grief Group Pitfalls

You might wonder why I am starting a discussion of grief groups with the pitfalls. However, many people make assumptions about grief groups just like they make assumptions about grief itself. They tend to view them very positively no matter if they are community groups, religious groups or groups held at local hospitals. Few people make any kind of distinction on whether the group is led by a grief professional or not, or whether they are well functioning. The assumption by most people is that any grief group is good but that is often not the case.

I think about that early scene in *Sleepless in Seattle* where Tom Hanks's friends are trying to comfort him after the loss of his wife, and one suggests he go to a grief group. He then picks up a pile of business cards he's been given by many well-meaning people that are for various grief groups. When I first watched that movie years before Tim died, I thought that was kind of funny that so many people tried to help him that way. However, I now realize how frustrating and unhelpful it really is.

So many people in your life, no matter if you are doing well or simply having a bad day, will suggest some grief group they heard about. Most of the time they really are trying to help but it's usually more irritating than helpful because they are suggesting you aren't handling things well, or at least not as well as they think you should. It's as if you suddenly aren't allowed to have a bad day for whatever reason. Everything is connected to your grief and their judgement of it.

I will be honest; I attended a grief group myself a few times. However, I quickly realized that not all groups are helpful and now that I've come much farther in my own journey, I can say some of them are truly detrimental. That doesn't mean you shouldn't try one. It just means that you need to do some due diligence and be sure the kind of group you attend will help you. There are some big red flags I am going to discuss that will allow you to determine if a group is right for you.

In my opinion, the most helpful kind of group is one that is forward focused. It is run by a grief professional, and the main goal is to help people progress as they grow and change.

In the first group I ever attended, I had an experience much like my friend, Debbie, in that the group members seemed stuck in the past. It was run by a layperson, not a professional counselor, and the few sessions I attended were depressing as people relived their trauma. I needed something more uplifting and encouraging, and this group did not fit that description. While I understand you have to face reality, to me it just seemed like torture for everyone. I couldn't understand why some of them had been coming for months or years.

When we first lose someone, I think all of us have a need to be with people who understand what we feel, so a grief group sounds logical. They understand the mood swings, the unpredictable behavior and the overwhelm that sets in from time to time. That is one of the best parts of a group.

However, if you are in a group that constantly talks about the pain and never advocates for its members to move forward and grow into their new life, you will be stuck in that same spot. It creates a group of very emotionally codependent people rather than a group that is trying to help each other through grief.

This is why I stopped going. I felt frustrated, and at times angered, that the person leading the group wanted people to rehash the pain rather than take actionable steps toward their future or talk about something positive.

In speaking with others who have attended different groups, a few also cautioned about religious groups. While religion can be a wonderful support system when you are grieving, there are some religious grief groups that pile on guilt and shame while you are trying to recover. In my opinion, there is no place in any group for guilt and shame. We feel what we feel and denying those feelings because someone thinks it's 'bad' is not helpful.

This is why I tell people to vet the groups they are thinking of joining in the following areas:

- Make sure the group is run by a professional grief counselor.

- Check to ensure (by attending a session or two) that it is forward focused and doesn't insist participants wallow in pain every session.

- Make sure your group is truly a safe place where you can share and not be judged.

- Get a feel for how long group members usually stay.

As with any grief group, it should not be a forever type of idea. We all move through grief at different speeds, but we should move through. Not getting stuck.

However, I don't want to discourage you from attending a grief group, just be sure you go in understanding what it can or can't do for you.

In an essence, I formed my own group of friends and people I met that have gone through the grief process. Their support has been vital to my own journey and though it was an informal group, in many ways I feel like it was as helpful to me as any formal group. I also spent months working one on one with a professional therapist which was a key factor in helping me to grow into a new life.

You Do You

No matter what path you choose, just understand that if you try a group or other avenue for help, and it doesn't work for you, don't be afraid to try something else. It is never a mistake to seek out those who can help you especially when you hit a rough patch and need to talk.

One area I want to address applies specifically to businesspeople and those with high profile jobs. One of the reasons I was very hesitant to share in a random grief group was the fact that my business is well known in my area. While we would all like to think, and may have even been told, that things shared in the group are private, most of us know that people will be people and things you say might be shared beyond the group. This is a huge risk and for this reason some people will not feel truly free to share.

I know there will be those that don't believe this happens or it didn't happen to them, but I am here to validate the concerns people have that information might be shared. It was a big concern for me at a time when the business my husband and I had built was vulnerable.

I was also vulnerable. That lack of trust was more about me than about any group I might be in, but it was still very valid. That is why, in my case, I felt that going to a grief professional who is legally obligated to keep my sessions private made more sense.

I know it may seem to be contradictory to say that now that I'm sharing the whole experience in a book, but it's not. Until I got through the majority of my own pain, I was very uncertain what I was comfortable with people knowing. My struggle led me to create this book in large part because so much of what I was told or understood about grief was completely wrong and that includes my understanding of grief groups.

It doesn't matter if you have a friend or family member that got tremendous good from their grief group, you still must decide if it's the best path for you. I will give you another example of this.

One of my friends, we'll call her Maggie, is a writer who is a widow. She also has a couple of NYT bestselling author friends, Ann and Rose, both of whom also experienced the death of a spouse. Maggie shared that the discussion about grief groups became a hot topic with her friends. They had high profile careers and professional personas they had to keep up. For all of them, this led to their circle of trusted confidants getting very small.

The idea that someone might share that they were struggling would have a detrimental effect on their business but that wasn't the only reason for concern. Just like me, they did not want unsolicited sympathy.

Many people are very private and for those who have suffered a loss, the constant reminder of that loss via unsolicited sympathy is very difficult to deal with. We don't want to talk about it with strangers at all, even those who are well-meaning.

When we are at our most vulnerable, our ability to trust anyone with that emotional journey lowers substantially.

These women did exactly as I did and sought very trusted long-time friends who had a similar experience to be their support during the grieving process.

Don't let anyone tell you your method of grieving is invalid.

For many people that serves much the same type of function as a formal grief group.

You may still choose to seek professional help, as I did, and I encourage anyone struggling with grief to do so. But don't let anyone tell you that your method of grieving, or which type of support you feel comfortable with, is somehow invalid or not 'good enough'.

That sort of judgement is completely out of line and no matter the process someone chooses, I applaud the fact they are trying to sort out their emotions and move forward.

For Maggie and her friends, that support of one another was equally as valuable, but that didn't mean people weren't constantly prodding them to go to one grief group or another. However, only you can determine what you need in the way of support and when you need it.

Growth Occurs in Hindsight

I am often asked how long grief takes. What people really want to know is how long it will take for them to feel like themselves again. I will tell you, as I tell them, there is absolutely no way to give a set time because every person is different, and every grief is different. There is also the fact that grief is never truly 'over'. It morphs and changes as we change but a small part of it will always be part of you.

I will share one point of interest and that is, while you are slogging through the emotional muck of grief you will constantly feel stuck. As if you haven't made any progress at all as your emotions ping pong from sad to angry to frustrated.

It is only after you have traveled through that muck for a while that you can look back and see that yes, you have made progress. Yes, you do feel more like your 'normal' self. Yes, there is hope.

One of my friends shared that for her, it was as if someone suddenly flipped a switch and she felt so much better. In her case, that was about two years after her husband died. For each of us the time frame is different but there will come a day you suddenly realize how much better you feel.

I would describe it as you wake up one day and the clouds part. That dark indescribable weight has lifted, and you don't feel that dark emotional weight that you've been carrying around month after month.

The mention of your loved one doesn't invoke extreme sadness and it's as if you've achieved enough emotional distance for it to be a part of your past rather than ever present each day, though that sadness will still happen on occasion.

I do believe that this is somewhat easier for those who have lives and jobs that are separate from their spouse. I didn't have my own separate identity from Tim. Our lives were completely intertwined in marriage, family, and business. There was no escaping the identity of 'we' no matter where I went or what I did. I had to rebuild my own identity from scratch on top of dealing with the loss of my spouse and I really struggled with that.

Everyone who loses a spouse loses part of their identity, that part where they are a couple and the life they shared with those who knew them as a couple. Everyone has to rebuild that part of their life as a single person so there's no escaping that. But when you also have to rebuild your professional life while at the same time worrying about money, the survival of the business and your employees on top of your own identity, well, let's just say it was overwhelming for me on occasion.

I am very grateful that I inherited a very strong will and emotional strength because I needed every bit of that to keep my professional life running as smoothly as possible while grappling with Tim's loss. When our professional lives and monetary success depend on us appearing strong and in control at all times, it is a big ask. Grief attacks your mind and spirit in so many ways, but I still had to get up, show up and work as so many people do.

As hard as that was, I think it saved me emotionally. I didn't have the time or luxury to fall apart or ignore our business. I had to force myself to continue and because of that I sought solutions. There were so many times I wanted to hide from life during that first year especially, but I couldn't.

Many of us must still provide for families and pay the bills no matter if our emotions are in tatters or not. As I look back now, I'm honestly stunned that I did hold things together at least enough to get through the worst of it. It seemed an insurmountable mountain at one time and to have come through that struggle and still create a joyful fulfilling life is the reward.

If you had told me the week, month or even first year after Tim's death that this type of life was possible, I would never have believed you as it seemed so far away. But step by step, putting one foot in front of the other, forcing myself to grow even when it was painful, it happened.

It will happen for you too.

We get no choice. If we love, we grieve.

– Thomas Lynch

Chapter 6

Second Year Blues

So many people who have lost a partner or spouse have told me that the second year was the hardest. I found that to be true in many ways as well. The reason is that the initial trauma subsides those first twelve months during which time, most people are just trying to maintain their lives. I focused so hard to getting through each day that the year passed with incredible speed. I think many of us are so preoccupied trying to keep it all together and get back to some semblance of normalcy, that we don't really process all the implications of what we have lost.

However, during that second year, the magnitude of the loss is amplified. The second year is when you realize this is real life and you have to start letting go of the old idea of your 'normal life'.

The loneliness and grief for the life you lost, not just the person you lost, hits hard. At the same time this is happening, the support you really need tends to subside. People are always there for you that first year, checking on you and worrying about you. But the second year, especially if you've spent the first year denying you need help (I'm FINE!), those people assume you are fine, and they go on about their lives.

Then you realize, they have a normal life to go back to, but you must build a new life from scratch, all by yourself. It can induce extreme sadness not to mention anger. Life shouldn't be this hard, you tell yourself. But it is and the only way through is to face it.

So many people find that year two is when they may really struggle with occasional bouts of depression when they really didn't that first year. This 'boomerang' depression is that grief for the life you must leave behind. The second year, you can easily go through all, or some, of the various stages of grief all over again and this is confusing and frustrating.

You Mourn More than the Person

For most people it takes a year or more for the realization that their life will never be the same to happen depending on how traumatic the death was in the first place. I think this occurred faster in my case simply because we spent almost every hour of the day together as spouses but also as business partners. So, I became very aware of the fact my life would never be the same about eight or nine months in. I desperately missed his friendship, his unwavering support, his business sense and not having any of that left me very empty and isolated.

I found it harder to accomplish the same amount of work and my productivity dropped no matter what I tried. At first, I really didn't get it because I have been a realtor for decades. It's not like I didn't know what to do or how to do it. But I found myself constantly exhausted and not just tired. I mean the kind of mental and physical exhaustion that doesn't go away. I finally realized that my relationship with Tim was what filled my energetic wellbeing both mentally and physically.

I took for granted the tremendous energy I got from our relationship and when he was no longer there, it took so much more effort for me to accomplish even the most mundane tasks. While I had been mourning the loss of Tim, I still needed to mourn the loss of the relationship and figure out what was next for me.

It is so easy to underestimate the power we get from certain relationships and how much they add to every part of our lives. We get so used to it being there, we don't even think about it and we never even try to imagine what life would be like without it. When that power left my life, it drained me in every way.

While I kept things rolling that first year through sheer force of will, by the end of that first year and beginning of the second year I had to admit to myself that things had to change. I had to lean more on other people and take more time for myself to figure things out. I still didn't like spending much time in the house or at our business because I felt the loneliness to such an intense degree.

I started spending more and more time at the beach house which I renovated that first year. We had used it as a rental property for a number of years so we really didn't spend a huge amount of time there. Because of that, it was one place I didn't connect with Tim so strongly. Even now as I write this book, I'm still spending a lot of time at the beach simply because it allows me to feel more like myself.

The urge to run away from home is very common.

Over the past few years, speaking to other people who are grieving, I've discovered that the urge to 'run away from home' is very common. But you can't do that forever. At some point you must confront those feelings and make some decisions. Are you going to keep the dream house now that the dream has changed? Will you downsize? Will you move to another city entirely?

I had to ask myself these same questions and face the truth that I would never be comfortable in the house we shared again. Other people who grieve make similar decisions. Some decide to pack their clothes and walk away from the house completely to start over. Others remodel the home to create that sense of connection with it once again. I want to emphasize that dealing with the home and furnishings is only one example of things you must confront by that second year if you haven't already.

One of the least talked about areas of concern that second year for many of us is financial, and it's a huge area! I went from two incomes to one overnight and I had to keep working. There was a big drop in my own income, not to mention missing Tim's income. That financial pressure is one of the hardest things to manage and even if your spouse plans ahead and leaves you in a good spot financially, you may still have the problem of other family members hovering around trying to claim part of those assets.

This can get very sticky, and it is so depressing that some people so quickly put a dollar value on a person. Legal disagreements over an estate can drag on for several years and this can add to the emotional stress you must continue to deal with.

The Isolation is Chilling

Something that is also common that second year is a more intense feeling of isolation. This happens to almost everyone who grieves simply because we tend to avoid those social engagements and events that first year. It's too hard to manage when we don't have much trust in our own emotions. We are just trying to get through it and avoiding those functions seems so much easier. But now that we've had a year away from social events, it can be very hard to reengage with that social environment.

You may feel as if so much has changed that you don't belong or fit in anymore since you used to attend those events as a couple. This means you must create new social connections and unfortunately, those take time, so we can become even more isolated.

As I grappled with forming a new idea of who I was, I also questioned if I wanted another relationship. That first year it was a definite no, I did not even want to think of it and the idea of starting over in the dating world seemed overwhelming. But by the second year I realized that I eventually wanted someone in my life. This is a very hard area to navigate at first when you've lost a spouse.

I found it hard not to feel like I was cheating on my husband and many people have those same emotions. I also hadn't been on a date since I was in college, so I wasn't even sure how or where to begin. I was slowly recreating my identity as a single woman and deciding what that meant as far as if, or when, I'd have another person in my life.

Part of the hesitancy I had toward a new relationship also included the fact that I still had what I would call 'grief storms' on occasion. These were times I'd cry myself to sleep over the smallest thing, and the next day be perfectly fine or I'd be extremely angry for absolutely no reason and then the anger leave as quickly as it appeared. I couldn't understand why I was still struggling on occasion with my emotions. I mean, shouldn't I be over it by now?

The answer to that is NO. As I previously discussed, grief isn't linear so your emotions don't necessarily follow any sort of accepted path. There were times that second year I was an emotional mess and it seemed to come right out of the blue. Now those happened less and less, but it seemed that every time I thought that I was finally over the worst part of grief, there it was again.

People often find this happens as they start to deal with the reality of how their life has changed. For example, you may be talking with a friend and the idea of retiring comes up. You picture yourself on the beach enjoying the sun with your spouse beside you and you may even talk about that.

Then you suddenly realize that those dreams and ideas you had about retiring aren't there anymore. It's not like you consciously thought about it since that person died, but it suddenly hits you that the visions you had as a couple about what your future would be simply won't happen - ever.

This is what I mean when I say that the magnitude of your loss really manifests in your mind that second year. That is because you are forcing yourself to create an identity, and a future, that does not include that person.

This is a big shift in mindset for a lot of us especially if your thoughts have included that person for most, or all, of your adult life. I talk a lot about a relationship being like a three-legged stool. You are one leg; your spouse is one leg and then the two of you as a couple are one leg and these three legs create your identity .

However, when you lose a spouse, you are in essence losing two of your three legs of identity – two thirds of who you are. People will often talk about losing your 'other half' but where your identity is concerned, you actually lose more than half. This is why creating that new part of your life is so hard and time consuming the second year.

You must create a life where you are a single person and not part of someone else. Let me tell you it is so much harder to be single than to be part of a couple, especially if you have been a couple for decades.

It often takes well past that first year for your mind to even catch up with the idea that you are now single. Every part of your life will be different now and that change is permanent, it's not going back to life as usual.

New Habits and Routines

Another reason that second year can be so challenging is that we don't necessarily take great care of ourselves that first year. When that second year rolled around for me, I had gained weight and wasn't feeling or looking my best and I knew it. Getting back into an exercise regime and taking care of yourself takes effort and by that second year you may have some health issues to unravel.

While we all know that exercise can be very good for our mental health, it is one more thing many of us avoid as we are trying to deal with our grief. A lot of my former exercise was in the form of golf with Tim or other couples or other activities that were social, which was the last thing I felt like participating in that first year.

Eating is another area that can be difficult. A lot of the time you spend with your partner or spouse probably revolves around meals. It did for us. It was the time we'd talk and laugh as we prepared a meal together in the kitchen or grilled out on the patio. Those were great memories, so I felt that void frequently.

I don't like cooking for one nor do I like eating out alone. Food can be an easy crutch to help us suppress emotions and get through the day. Wine was my friend as well. Both of these things packed pounds on me quickly and I had little desire to deal with it. But eventually, as with all areas of grief, I had to face it. I had to establish new routines and new patterns of living if I was going to get healthy and stay that way. This is true in all areas of your life, and it becomes much more evident that second year.

We must develop new ways of doing things, new patterns, new reasons to move forward. The motivation to continue on without your loved one can come and go at times. That is part of the melancholy many of us feel on occasion that second year.

As we face the realization of creating a life without them, we often ask ourselves why? Why do I want to go on without them and what is there for me now? We have to find something to look forward to rather than merely existing because that's not enough.

Certain dates and occasions can bring up that sad feeling as well. Tim's birthday, our anniversary and the date of his death are all within a few weeks of each other and I had a period of sadness during that time the second year, and every year since.

Expect the Second Wave

I believe that the reason so many people struggle that second year after losing a loved one is that second year grief is so unexpected. Especially if you navigate that first year relatively well, those second year blues can come as a surprise.

I believe the fact that it is talked about so little is a detriment to all of us who go through grief. In order to effectively handle emotional obstacles in my life, I like to have some kind of idea that they are there or might be coming my way. When you acknowledge the idea of second year grief, then you are much more likely to handle it better. You are prepared in some sense, so it doesn't catch you so off guard. In most of the grief books I looked to for answers they didn't spend hardly any time talking about many of these issues which is why I am spending so much time acknowledging and addressing them.

The issues of second year grief as well as the difficult task of figuring out who you are now can't be overstated in my opinion. The trauma of a loved one's death will subside, but that doesn't mean grief is over or that you won't struggle in some way as you try to move forward.

As I have said many times, everyone experiences grief differently and that is true for the second year as well. Some struggle intensely, others only have the occasional issue. However, from the people I have talked to and my own experience, I can say the vast majority have encountered unexpected problems that second year. While you may be fortunate enough not to experience some of these issues yourself, I hope this will give you a great deal more compassion and understanding for those that do.

Not everyone who reads a book about grief is dealing with grief themselves. Many times, the person reading is a friend or loved one of someone who is struggling with grief. Explaining how grief manifests itself and how different it can be for each individual will hopefully give all of us much more understanding of those who are grieving.

As I said at the beginning of this book, I had absolutely no idea how grief can affect someone who has lost a spouse until I experienced it. I was one of those who thought they knew how grief was supposed to go. I knew it had stages and I assumed that you go through those stages, and then you are yourself again.

Only now do I realize how wrong I was. You are never 'yourself' again because the person you were when you experienced that trauma of loss and the person you are afterward are never the same. Grief changes you, teaches you, and shows you how fragile our lives are.

Grief shows you how fragile our lives are.

While I believe there is still a great life ahead after loss, that doesn't mean everyone gets there quickly or easily. It takes work and that work is hard. Nothing about life after loss is ever easy and I don't want to give the impression that it is.

However, I have found the journey to be one that helped me put the past in perspective and understand who I am on a much deeper level. That has tremendous value.

Tears are the silent language of grief.

— **Voltaire**

Chapter 7

Family Grief

The idea of family grief isn't new, but for those who are grieving it's not really something they may have thought about before it happened to them. So it's important to understand that it matters if you are the spouse, child, parent, sibling, or close friend of the person who passed as it will determine how that grief manifests in your life. Your relationship with that person, and the people who loved them, will also affect the way you grieve.

To say it's a hot mess of family stress is probably an understatement. Grief is one of those times when everyone has heightened emotions and relationships can easily deteriorate or cease to exist after a death due to hurt feelings or misunderstandings. The fact that we all grieve differently is one of the causes of that stress. It's like we expect to all experience things in the same way, so we may be much less understanding if a family member doesn't process their grief in the same way we do.

For example, you may have the experience, as I did, of adult children who expect your life and family traditions to remain the same. As a grown child it can give them comfort to feel as if that loss is honored by nothing changing. However, as a spouse, that can be tortuous! You may feel judged or trapped by the past and that others aren't embracing your desire to move forward.

I'm going to talk about various ways that family grief may show itself and give you some examples so you will know it when you see it. While friends and coworkers grieve too, it's just different with family. It is so much more intense and while friends and coworkers come and go in your life, you must find a way to deal with family for the long term.

I will be giving you some tools to help with family grief in this chapter too. It is critical that you think about these tools and be ready to use them as soon as you see those stress warning signs. While you may be deep into your own grief, family will still rely on each other for support to get through those darkest days and being prepared is the best way to successfully navigate what can be a very traumatic time for you all.

Managing Family Grief Expectations

Just as we all have assumptions of what grief is or how it progresses, we also assume that the focus of grief is on the individual. Very little is written or said about how the family dynamic effects grief. However, most of what we learn in regard to dealing with grief comes from family and our past experience. It is influenced by culture, religion, and expectations of family members.

For example, in some families, it is expected that they fall apart and weep uncontrollably both at the funeral and for a long time after. If someone doesn't follow this pattern, the rest of the family talks about them or wonders if they are 'really grieving'. The same is true of very stoic families and I fall into this category. The expectation in my family was always, suck it up, don't let people see you cry or show weakness. If someone does fall apart in public, they might be frowned upon by other family members or made to feel weak.

Let me say this again, there is no right or wrong way to grieve but these family expectations can add to our stress if our grief doesn't conform to their expectations. We don't even realize we carry these ideas of grief around until we are knee deep in it and trying to grapple with those feelings of inadequacy because our emotions aren't following some imaginary script.

When we move past the event of death and try to start piecing our lives back together, everything has changed for the whole family even if you don't realize it yet. It takes varying amounts of time for each family member to come to that realization and no one can rush it for anyone else. This means that family members are moving ahead at a different pace and that can cause even more stress than the actual death did sometimes. It can also cause irreparable harm if that stress leads to a family rift.

You'd think that shared loss would bring family closer and sometimes it does with a lot of good communication and work. However, it can also cause a deep chasm between family members who need different things in order to get through their own grief. Let me give you an example.

When adult children grieve, they often find comfort in talking nonstop about how great their parent was and all the good times they remember. That's a good thing for them as they are expressing their emotions by talking it through. However, the widowed parent of those adult children may find it devastating to constantly talk about their spouse, especially at first, because every conversation takes them right back to that moment of traumatic death. It also prevents them from feeling like they can move forward without that spouse, yet they must.

This tends to lead to family members avoiding each other because they can't stand to deal with the others' way of grieving. It happens so easily especially when no one knows enough about grief to understand what is going on.

It is important to realize from the outset that a death in the family will change the family dynamic no matter what. The roles of each family member shift, maybe slightly at first, but over time they change dramatically.

Maybe that person, who everyone leaned on for advice and support, is no longer there. Someone else must fill that role and everyone will feel lost for a time. Individual differences in grieving can also lead to some feeling smothered with family 'help' and others feeling left out or suddenly alone. Things are awkward for a while as no one really is sure who will fill what role.

This can be compounded if one person decides to fill that role or responsibility in the family where others don't agree it's their role. I can't even tell you the number of widows especially, who have had a grown child suddenly decide to try to take over their finances and their life as if they can no longer decide anything for themselves. It's as if they don't recognize you can take care of yourself at all and set about trying to 'help' you to the point of dictating your life.

Communication is really the key.

We often don't really give a lot of thought to how our grown children, or other family members, perceive our relationships. They haven't lived our lives and may perceive that one or the other spouse was in 'charge' and so jump into that assumed role having no idea what you want or need.

Communication is really the key here. Rather than allowing them to see their parent as a helpless grieving widow or widower, it is important to tell your family what you need and what you don't. While this is uncomfortable at first, and likely to change over time, that is the only way they will know. Assumptions get all of us in trouble and managing the expectations of family grief, and the resulting change in family dynamics, is all about communicating needs.

I'm not saying there is a quick or easy solution. There are good tools but even with the best of intentions, there will still be tension at times. There will still be drama. There will still be the disagreement on occasion. But that is normal.

You are creating a new family from the old and that transition will have its bumps and hiccups no matter what. Only you can keep those lines of communication open so when, not if, those tensions arise you can work through them together.

Before we get into talking about family healing through grief, I want to stress that grief is something we each carry alone. As a parent, especially as a mom, I know what its like to want to take that burden of grief off your child's shoulders. To try and make things easier or better for them. But you can't. We each must travel through grief at our own pace and in our own way and there's nothing you can do to change that.

I think we all try so hard to be accommodating when the whole family is stressed, but often that attempt at accommodation leads to more tension later. Open, honest communication is important even if the truths that need to be said, or the emotions that need to be worked through, are very difficult. Putting it off or trying to soften the blow causes more pain later. You can't lesson someone else's pain.

I also want to acknowledge that not everyone has a supportive family during grief. Family dynamics that are already strained, or even shattered, before a death can become much more intense afterward.

The best you can do in those situations is brace yourself and understand that it will pass. That doesn't mean things will be better, but you will be able to choose if you continue those relationships or not.

Family Healing – The Beginning

In order to start healing as a family, it is important to discuss some very basic ideas about grief and to discuss those together. Even if it's been a while since your loved one passed, and your family has already experienced some difficulty, there is no time like the present to set things right.

Step 1: Open Communication

The most important thing to get across to everyone is the understanding that grief is messy and there will be issues and tension. That allows everyone to know that you all expect there will be problems and you aren't going to brush them aside or ignore those concerns just because it's difficult or hard.

When talking about those emotions the biggest ones I'd start with are frustration and patience. Because we all grieve differently it can be extremely hard not to get frustrated with other family members who are either grieving differently than we are or who are wanting to talk about things that are extremely hard for us.

It can feel like they are wanting their grief to trump ours or are assuming their needs are more important. That is not it at all, usually. We are all feeling big emotions and for some that means talking about it constantly whereas others want to avoid it completely. Neither one is wrong.

It takes an extreme amount of patience to work through those emotions and those differences. Even as a parent of adult children I can tell you that frustration can build to almost intolerable levels. Especially if other family members are judging how you are handling things or are wanting to push their idea of how your life should progress onto you.

It is completely normal when we are stressed to withdraw from the conflict and avoid it. But that doesn't help or work long-term. You must manage your own frustration while having the patience to keep the lines of communication open. It is so much harder to repair later if you let that communication get completely severed. Again, talking about frustration and patience as a family as early as possible manages those expectations.

Step 2: Acknowledge We All Grieve Differently

Once you open the discussion with family about grief, it's important to talk about the fact of how different grief is and that there is no 'right' way. Grief manifests in so many ways from complete avoidance to negative or harmful addictions. It runs the gambit from family members who may seem overly happy to those who are sarcastic and lash out in a nasty or hurtful way. Some want other people around; others need alone time to process their own grief.

There will always be those who don't want to talk about grief or don't believe grief will affect them in any of those ways. I was one of those I suppose. I kept thinking if I could keep going and not acknowledge my own emotions they would get back in line like good little soldiers and no one would know any different. But that didn't happen.

There will be those who deny their own grief for extended periods and, like me, they struggle more the second year than the first. By that time other family members are well along in their own grieving process and may get frustrated that some are just now starting. But that is part of it, which leads to step 3.

Step 3: Respect Everyone's Grief Process and Timeline

I will tell you this is a tough one. Its human nature to compare ourselves to others including family. We point out our differences or perception that someone isn't doing things as we think they should all the time and that includes during grief. This is especially true as people try to reform family dynamics and move forward with new lives.

Openly talking about the fact that we are all different and deserving of respect will keep that negative chatter to a minimum, though it may still happen. Family talking about each other in a negative way is where many of the hurt feelings come from so guard your own conversations and encourage family to do so as well. This one simple thing can help you avoid having to address more hurt later.

Lack of respect for everyone's grief process can also quickly shut down communication or make some family members feel like their emotions aren't worthy of discussing. While we all must process our grief individually, the whole family is navigating unfamiliar territory together so even if you don't necessarily understand another family member's grief, you can exhibit patience and kindness as they work through it.

I do want to go back and touch on the grief timeline here as well. When there is a traumatic or unexpected death, everyone starts the grief process at the same point. However, if there has been an extended illness, for example cancer, Alzheimer's, or similar illness, some family members may have started grieving at the diagnosis so have had months or even years to think through their grief and feelings.

Other family members may not start grieving for that person until the actual death occurs so there can be a large disparity in grieving timelines which can cause increased tension.

Even when a death is sudden some family members will go through their process faster than others and this difference in timeline can once again cause frustration. It is important to understand that even the most well-adjusted person may have bouts of grief that pop up years later seemingly out of nowhere, so none of us are immune to an extended grief timeline.

Step 4: Feel the Feels

What is it about emotion that makes so many of us want to run and hide? I'm not really sure the answer to that, I just know it does. When death is involved, those feelings can get complicated and sticky. As a family, it's important to make it okay to feel all the feelings even if some of those are difficult.

No one is a saint and dying doesn't suddenly make them one. However, it is very common for family members to refuse to hear anything negative about their loved one after death.

Each family member had a different relationship with the person who passed and some of those relationships or memories probably weren't positive. Each family member has to be allowed to work through those messy emotions or deal with the fact that things they wanted to say will never be said. That isn't easy.

The issues that exist before death don't disappear.

It's not easy for them to feel those emotions and its not easy for you to hear them. But they exist and denying them only alienates family at this point.

This is an area that can really divide siblings when a parent dies. Each child in a family has a vastly different relationship to their parent and that contrast becomes very evident after the parent dies.

The issues that exist before death don't disappear for those left behind. Neither is there any resolution at that point, which means they have to learn to live with what did, or didn't, happen and somehow put that in the past.

Ensuring that conversations with family are a safe space for people to share their emotions is very important to moving forward as a family. Patience and kindness is key to getting through those hard times and working through emotions even when there are no resolutions to be had.

Step 5: Healthy Boundaries

Grief changes over time for each person and it's important to know what you can give emotionally and what you can't, and when. There may be a time when you can't talk about it or would simply prefer not to. Later, as you process more, you may be able to have those conversations more easily.

Communicating your own boundaries at various time will allow you to head off many tensions that may arise. A simple, "I know this is so hard for you, its hard for me too and my emotions are drained today. I want to be able to hear you, so can we talk about this tomorrow maybe?"

When we are at a low spot, it can be so very hard to hear someone else's emotions. However, you have to communicate that and let them know you care, but are at your emotional limit at that second. This is also true if the timing is awkward.

Because I work with family, it was not unusual for someone to want to talk about their struggles right in the middle of the business day after Tim died. Honestly, I could not do that and still hold it together the rest of the day to do my job. I had to communicate that boundary: that I valued hearing them out but needed to be able to do that when I could handle it better emotionally.

You might at first feel that setting these boundaries is pushing people away, but its not. You are acknowledging their needs while also stating your own and that is a good thing. Respecting each other's boundaries and emotional bandwidth at any time during the grieving process allows you to all move forward together supporting each other.

Family is the Best – and THE WORST

While some people have supportive families in times of grief, others don't, and I wanted to talk about that fact with as much openness and honestly as I can. I have seen and heard some awful things that happen in families when someone dies. Many of these I've heard from people as I talk to them about grief, but also in my profession as a realtor, as assets are divided up. I've seen some truly horrible family dynamics.

Many of these issues come up in blended families as family members try to get what they perceive to be their rightful share while also inflicting as much emotional trauma as possible on each other. I've seen family fights and estates end up in court, siblings never speak to one another again, and families basically ripped apart forever when a death happens.

I put a lot of thought into what I would tell someone who was in that situation and my own advice is: *save yourself.* There is absolutely nothing you can do about the way people behave or what they choose to focus on when someone dies. You can't save them or change them or insist they do things your way. At some point, you must realize it is what it is and all you can do is protect yourself.

That is easier said than done I know, and I've heard tales of grown children emptying houses, bank accounts and tying things up in court leaving the widow or widower destitute. I've seen grandparents cut off grandchildren or stepchildren over their hurt and anger after a death. I've also seen family refuse to accept someone moving on, dating again or even remarrying to the point they cut off all contact.

Again, there is nothing you can do about those circumstances other than deal with them in a way that protects you both physically and emotionally. This is way beyond the idea of 'setting boundaries'. That only works with supportive loving families. If you have hostile family members that are set on doing you financial or emotional harm, the best course of action is to get away from them and protect yourself.

I think there is some idea, especially if you have 'gotten along' with those family members for years, that you are under some kind of obligation to have a relationship with them. But that is not true. I've heard a widow say she tried because her deceased husband would have wanted her too. I don't agree. If those grown children or family members had acted that way when he was alive, he'd have cut them off himself. Even so, you are under no obligation to continue to expose yourself to emotional harm (or financial or physical harm) out of a sense of duty. Not only will it devastate you emotionally it can put you in significant danger.

It is okay to let go if things are bad. You are not supposed to carry the weight of the universe on your shoulders nor try to fix the broken people in your life. The hard part is knowing where to draw the line and only you can do that.

The Opposite of Positive Coping

Even with the best supportive family many of us engage in what I can only describe as extremely negative coping when we are grieving. Some of these are more extreme than others, but all have one root cause: avoidance of pain.

Of course, there is no such thing as really avoiding the pain, but we try. I did this by pretending everything was fine. I was fine, the family was fine, the business was fine. It wasn't fine, and by trying to hold things together I delayed the inevitable pain.

I also exhibited other negative coping behaviors: I ate too much. I drank too much. I had a terrible case of gallows humor and inappropriate outbursts. None of these things helped me at all or fooled anyone really, they only delayed the grief.

> # We avoid until we can't anymore and then we fall apart.

We all engage in any kind of coping we can to get through those horrible first days, weeks and months. We avoid until we can't anymore and then we fall apart. Once that bout of emotion wanes, we do it all again. It is the back and forth that is so exhausting and in the middle of that exhaustion is overwhelm. I was overwhelmed in so many ways but in others, I sailed right along. I was able to work effectively for clients and keep things going business wise but could not spend Sunday nights alone for the longest time.

At the time it felt as if I was losing my mind and now as I look back on it, it must have seemed so to the people who were close to me! I felt in control and 'normal' in some areas of life and like an awkward, unsure preteen in others.

As I researched things for this book, the idea of avoidance was a big topic because I recognized it so readily through my own grief. What I discovered is that the underlying root of avoidance is really fear. Fear you will really go crazy. Fear you will be embarrassed or lose control. Fear you will never get back any sort of happiness in your life.

When death first happens, these fears overwhelm your emotions. Then, as time progresses, you face that overwhelm in waves as you develop the coping skills to adjust to life without your loved one.

That doesn't mean those emotions go away, but you prove to yourself over time that all is not lost. That you are able to handle those emotions and still function. That life, though drastically changed, does indeed go on.

There is no doubt that some refuse to develop any coping skills and descend into avoidance even farther with substance abuse or even thoughts of suicide. No matter the stage you are in or the overwhelm you face, there is always help via a qualified grief counselor.

I took this route myself when I realized months into my grieving process that I wasn't moving ahead as I wanted. I always tell people to get help sooner rather than later even if they aren't sure.

If you show up at the grief counselor for no other reason than to hear a rational person tell you that you aren't crazy, that has value so don't wait.

Grief is just love with no place to go.

– Jamie Anderson

Chapter 8

Starting Life
Again

*F*or all of us that travel the road of grief, there is a distinct 'before' and 'after'. You are not the same. You will never be the same and life will change as you navigate your grief. However, there will come a time when you feel as if you are ready to make positive forward change in your life and the question then becomes, What now?

Sometimes that change means moving to a new area or changing where you live. It can also mean a new relationship or new friend group. While it is a relief for many of us to feel we have progressed in our grief journey, the idea and reality of moving on can bring up a myriad of emotions we may not expect. These emotions not only come from us, as we awkwardly and hesitantly find our way, but they can also come from family members, friends, and others.

Not every widow/widower or divorced person wants a new relationship and sometimes that fact is harder for people to accept than if you had already moved into a new relationship. It may sound a little crazy but there are many people who really embrace being single especially after having a long relationship in the past. They don't need, or want, to go there again.

On the other side of the coin are those who do realize they want to have someone in their life again. I am in this category so I will speak from personal experience on this subject. But no matter which camp you fall into, there will be uncertainty about if you should be going this direction and even if you do feel you are going the right direction, how do you navigate the path?

I will say that trying to fit an additional person into a family unit that has lost someone is difficult under the best of circumstances. Even if you are a long way from that milestone, your mind goes right to that point. This is why dating after grief is so intimidating. If you do find someone and you do hit if off, what would your family even call that person? Grandma's boyfriend? It can't help but feel extremely awkward.

There is no simple or easy way to approach reimagining your life and the idea that everyone will support you and understand how you want to live your life is misplaced. They won't understand and you must prepare yourself to live your life in the way that best suits you no matter what. Over time, things will improve with good communication but when situations get difficult, and they will, you must have a firm resolve to live your own life. Now let's talk about that life.

It's Awkward

I have never been the kind of person that likes to eat alone at a restaurant. After my husband died, I often ate out with friends but when I went out alone, I would find myself eating at the bar rather than a table. This was my preference and there are many of you who probably have no issue eating alone but it was really one of the first areas in my life where I felt the awkwardness of now being single.

It sticks out in my mind as one of those situations I'm still not completely comfortable with and while it's not a huge thing, it was the beginning of my learning how to live this new life for myself.

I am a very social person, as are many realtors! It wasn't but about a year after Tim died that I realized I wanted someone in my life. No, I wasn't looking for a replacement for the relationship because it is something you can't ever replace. However, I like having a close male friend that I can go places with, do activities with and have that companionship. Over a few months, I met and spent time with a widower who understood a lot of what I was experiencing because he was going through the same thing. We had a lot in common and enjoyed each other's company.

That doesn't mean it wasn't awkward! It was for both of us. It is very common when you have been married a long time to somehow feel as if you are cheating on your spouse when you spend time with someone new.

Of course, you know in your mind that's ridiculous, but your heart feels something different. I had to work through those feelings while also dealing with family members and friends who felt as if I was abandoning Tim's memory or moving too quickly.

I found other people's expectations to be very frustrating. I was already dealing with my own awkwardness trying to navigate dating and really did not need their input, but that didn't stop them. In some ways other people were the easiest to deal with, but my own emotions and feelings were another story.

Through the lessons I learned in my horrible awkwardness, there are a few truths that I want you to grasp as you try to navigate the creation of your new life. We will come back to the idea of getting through the awkward at the end of the chapter but first, the five truths.

The Five Truths of Moving Forward

Truth #1: Moving Forward Doesn't Mean Forgetting

This is the hardest idea to really grasp at first. When the initial grief hits, your emotions are all about your loved one. They are intense and the idea that you could change or make positive headway doesn't even seem possible. However, as time passes, your mind and heart begin to heal from the initial trauma and while the love for your loved one will always be there, it doesn't limit your capacity to love or change your life.

For whatever reason, many people have the idea that in order to love another person you must somehow delete the previous person from your memory which is absolute nonsense. Its as if we want to limit our world to this tiny box and for someone else to join our box, we must kick the feelings for a former love out. Somehow when it comes to adding a new partner, friend or spouse after a death, we often experience intense guilt or shame as if that former love is being replaced.

Moving forward isn't an either/or scenario. It's a both/and type of life where you remember and honor the good in the past while freely embracing the good your life can hold now. That doesn't mean you won't experience some of those negative emotions of guilt or shame as you try to navigate your new world. Those are normal and will diminish as you embrace the life you want.

Truth #2: Grief Doesn't Magically End

Even when you are fully convinced you are ready to step into a new life or new relationship, that doesn't mean you won't experience waves of grief on occasion. Grief can and does arise at the most unexpected times, even years down the road, no matter how far you feel you've come. As we talked about in previous chapters, the grief gets molded into who we are, it never completely goes away.

There will always be times, even years later, that we may long for what was and that's okay. It is also true that there may be some parts of grief we aren't ready to feel until significant time has passed. Grief is extremely complex and there is no one path for each person. Even as you move forward, you will always carry the experience of grief with you but it doesn't have to stop you or prevent you from living a very full life.

> There will always be times, even years later, that we long for what was.

An example of this for me occurs on occasion when social media shows those events from years past. I ignored this completely at first because I didn't want to be plunged right back into the trauma, so I avoided it. *Delete, delete, delete.*

However, by avoiding it completely I was not allowing myself to embrace those good times and heal from the hurt.

I explain it to others by saying its somewhat like very slowly ripping the bandage off a painful would. As time goes on, you are willing to feel a little of that pain so you can move on. As you peel back more of the hurt and allow yourself to feel those emotions, you get to that place of healing where you aren't as afraid of the pain and can embrace those remembered good times fully.

A couple of years after Tim died, one of those photo memories popped up on my phone yet again. It was a photo of us a few weeks before we got his diagnosis, and he had the surgery. I saw us in that picture so happy and completely unaware that anything was wrong or that a few months later Tim would be dead, and I'd be alone. My heart squeezes with hurt a little even now as I think about it. We were so unaware that life would never be the same.

This time, when that picture popped up, I knew it was time to feel that pain and I wanted to. Because without feeling the pain and healing, I couldn't embrace the happiness that we'd shared which was reflected in that photo. It didn't matter that I was in another relationship or that I'd moved on in so many ways. There were, and still are, times when a wave of grief for my husband, or for our old life, will wash over me. It happens and may continue to all my life. That is the reality of grief.

Truth #3: You Define Your Life

One of the hardest parts of trying to move forward are all the people in your life who try to tell you what you need and what you don't. They have expectations of what you should and shouldn't do, who you should and shouldn't associate with, and how your life should proceed. While this is very difficult to deal with on occasion, you must get to the place where you can put your wants, needs and desires for your own life above their opinions.

This will cause tension in the relationships, no doubt, but its not your job to make everyone else happy. In fact, you can't and even in trying to please others you will make yourself miserable. Its even harder when you have depended and relied on some of these same people to get through that first year because they now feel as if you are their responsibility, but you aren't.

This truth also includes that idea that no one has a set timeline for grief or for moving forward. Your life may change quickly and dramatically when you decide you are ready, or it may move at a slow steady pace while you heal. There is no right way or right answer and its important to communicate with those other people in your life to ensure you have good emotional boundaries with them.

You don't 'owe' anyone anything in regard to how you want to live now, and they must accept it. It takes quite a bit of strength to stand up for yourself when you've spent so long feeling completely broken and unsure of your own emotions. However, you can and will do it.

Truth #4: Self Care is Vital

I've already talked a bit about how important it is to take care of yourself as you grieve, but this is especially true as you try to move forward. I have found it very helpful to focus on inundating myself with positive actions and activities. Things like exercise, golf, getting together with friends and others who are finding life after grief.

It is common, as time goes on and everyone else goes back to their 'normal' life, for isolation and depression to set in even if it's been a couple of years since the death. It is normal for you to feel disconnected from your old life and old routines and to move on, you must take an active role in creating new routines that are positive.

Perhaps you join a club or group with a similar interest or take some exercise classes. It doesn't matter what it is as long as it is positive and gets you reconnecting with people as soon as you feel the least bit ready. That timeline is up to you, not anyone else.

You'd think that self-care of any kind would be viewed as positive, however I can tell you that getting a makeover, buying a few new clothes and going out with friends can be viewed negatively by some in your life, especially siblings/family of the deceased or grown children. It's not that they don't love you necessarily, it is often because they hold on to the way things were as a way for them to feel close to their deceased parent or loved one. Once you start to change, or dare to look happy, they may view it as abandoning that memory.

As with every part of grief, keeping those lines of communication open is the only way to get through those type of tensions. It will not be perfect but keeping everything the same isn't right either. Things aren't the same and everyone in your life must eventually face that reality. You aren't responsible for their grief or how it progresses (or doesn't).

Truth #5: You Can't Make Things Perfect

No matter what you do or how you do it in your journey to move forward, someone in your life will judge you. The absolute best thing you can do for yourself, and for others in your life, is to live as you see fit. They will adjust, or they won't, but you can't put your life on hold waiting for them to catch up.

Your life can, and will, be equally as good as it was before or better depending on the circumstances, but only if you embrace the change that comes with it. By change, I mean not only the outward changes of how you live but also the inward change in you as a person.

We don't often think of grief as a journey of personal growth, but it absolutely is. I have learned so much about myself that I might have never learned had Tim not died when and how he did. I have become so much more compassionate and understanding of others in every respect as well. Its not that I wasn't compassionate before, it is just that grief gives you such a depth of understanding and empathy for people.

> We all travel this grief journey together, but separately.

Part of that understanding is letting go of any kind of perfectionist mindset. No matter how perfect someone's life may seem, I guarantee you that it is not. Feeling and showing our own vulnerabilities and imperfections allows others to let their guard down and connect in ways I had no idea about before. I now strive for that connection as I know its real, whereas I wasn't even aware of it before.

It is so very important to understand that you can't fix everything (or anything really). You can't erase the grief from yourself, or others, and you can't make it easier. You must teach yourself to let go of those things instead and allow everyone to find their own way, including you.

Forcing a pretend façade out of guilt, shame, or denial will never work, and everyone will see through that tough exterior sooner rather than later. No matter how much you want to get past grief or how hard you try to be 'perfect' you aren't, and everyone will see that.

For me personally, I don't want things to ever be perfect for me again in the way I once imagined simply because I know that is not where the best part of life resides. Living a full, loving, purposeful life is about embracing that imperfection and building something good with it. I know I will continue to experience the occasional wave of grief for Tim and that's okay. Its part of my journey and always will be. That doesn't make me less than, or better than, anyone else who has ever experienced grief.

We all travel this grief journey together, but separately, and that is how it has to be. Time doesn't heal all for everyone and there will still be unresolved issues with your loved one no matter what. However, you get to choose what you hold on to and what you let go of. Even if some of your family or friends hold on to old hurts or unresolved arguments, you don't have to. You are completely in control of your healing.

Back to Awkward

I can't even express the angst and uncertainty that arises when you finally decide you want to create a new life. While at first, your mind may be completely blank as to where to start, within a short time, most people find themselves overwhelmed with options. This is a good thing!

When you are ready to meet new people or try new things, there are a few ideas I have for you that might make it easier. Some of these tips are dos, some are don'ts, but with either one, you decide for yourself what might fit your life.

The good news about redefining your life now is that there are no rules, and nothing is set in stone. You may try one of these ideas and decide it doesn't work for you and that's fine. Pick another! The more you try things, the less awkward you will feel and the more confidence you will gain in moving forward.

I do want to focus on confidence first. Recreating a friend group or joining a social group boosts your confidence and that is one thing that is vital for you to gain as you step out into the future. Confidence is everything and other people feel that confidence.

When we go through grief, we often become very good at hiding our emotions or disguising how we feel. This can make anyone seem shy and reserved when really, you may only be uncertain or unsure. This is normal, but if you are aware of it, you can combat what may be a negative first impression others have of you.

It will take a while for you to feel like 'yourself' again and be able to show joy, or really laugh and enjoy others, without reservation. I was self-conscious and very aware of who was around me for a very long time. I felt guilty for having 'too much' fun or even being happy! I imagined I was being judged, by others, by myself, by friends and family.

As time passed, I realized that wasn't true. It was still awkward to feel, and show, those normal emotions but just like anything that is awkward at first, when you do it often enough it once again goes back to feeling normal.

I am going to list a few dos that will help you get started connecting with others. These are only suggestions, but hopefully they will help you think of other ideas that will work for you, too.

Do:

- **Go out in groups** – This is much less pressure filled and allows you to focus on being part of an ensemble rather than carrying on a conversation one on one.

- **Join a group with a shared interest (hobby) that does not know the deceased** - This allows you to focus on fun rather than have yet another conversation about grief.

- **Meet new people and form new friendships** – One of the hardest areas to navigate are the friends that knew you both. By meeting new people and forming new friendships you will feel more freedom to be yourself.

- **Positive distraction** – Engage in those activities that bring you joy whether that is something like reading, sports or gardening. Even if you do these activities completely alone, they allow you to spend your time in a positive joyful way.

- **Go to events you enjoy** - This might include concerts, art shows or sporting events. This will bring you into contact with people who have similar interests.

Don't:

- **Sit home alone** – You know when you need to get out even if it is just to take a walk. Sitting in a depressed or lonely state will only bring more of that so its up to you to break the cycle and take control of how you feel.

- **Feel you have to have family approval** – This includes not only where you go but who you meet. Friends and family who knew the loved one who passed will inevitably make comparisons and that's really not fair to you or the new person in your life.

- **Meet people online** – I'll insert a quick caveat here. This is not so much a 'don't' as it is me encouraging you to be extremely cautious. I know several widows and widowers who have met people online and are very happy. However, this can also be a pit as few people are truly how they appear online, and some (many) are complete con artists. When you are grieving you need to meet real, genuine people and the online world is not the best place to do it. When you are vulnerable, it can be very easy to get taken advantage of in one way or another.

- **Create unrealistic expectations** – Yes, we all make comparisons to our old life and that is normal but bringing unrealistic expectations to something new may destroy your own path forward. You must let go of the past and allow things to unfold naturally.

These are extremely short lists to get you started but I'm sure you get the idea. Having the right mindset, and not allowing others to tell you how you feel, is critical to getting past that awkward stage.

While no one chooses to grieve, it allows us to grow and reshape who we are and who we choose to be going forward. Only you can make these decisions for yourself but once you do, a wonderful and fulfilling life awaits.

How lucky am I to have something that makes saying goodbye so hard.

— Winnie the Pooh

Chapter 9

The Worst Part of Grief

I thought a lot about what I consider to be the very worst part of grief. Many areas you travel through as you grieve are truly difficult and it's not necessarily about one being worse than the other as they all have their struggles. However, in my opinion, the hardest area of grief for most of us is continued acceptance. It sounds easy, right? You know someone you loved has died or is no longer in your life. Its reality and its common to think that mentally or intellectually accepting that reality is enough. But it's not.

When we are talking about grief, acceptance is a long process. Acknowledging and accepting a loved one's physical absence is just the start. It is much more difficult to accept and adapt to the changes in every single area of your life that you didn't think about at first.

My life had a set rhythm prior to Tim's death. It was a lifestyle and collection of habits/norms that I didn't even consciously think about. That life was created over the better part of four decades and made up the secure, worry-free life I lived. Once my husband was no longer there, that security blanket I'd always taken for granted, and those habits, were immediately gone. It seemed that everything, every single thing, took a herculean effort in a way it never had before.

I could accept that he was gone. I could accept that my life would change. But I had a very hard time understanding and accepting that the normal rhythm of my life would never return no matter what I did. I remember a few occasions sitting on my bed and ugly crying my eyes out. It was so freaking hard! I wondered if I was somehow making it harder because there were times I thought the longing for my old life might crush me. I thought there was no way it could be this hard for other people. But it is.

My anger would resurface when things got especially difficult. I felt as if I had no control over so many things that were not even an issue when Tim was alive. Many people feel this type of long-term struggle with acceptance as the after effects of the loss of that person sets in.

I've talked to many partners who have lost a spouse through death, long term illness, or even to divorce, and there are some common themes and questions that arise in this regard. I'm going to present them in this chapter as a question and answer. Understand that my answers come from my own experience and the experiences of those I have interviewed and spoken with directly. These are not theoretical mental health ideas, but comments from others who have experienced this type of loss personally.

Will I ever feel like I belong again?

It was a shock to me to feel awkward and out of place in my own life, but I did, and many people feel this almost immediately. It's as if all those connections with friends, family and coworkers are suddenly severed. In reality, the relationships aren't so much severed as instantly changed which feels like the same thing. Our minds assume nothing has changed and we have this strong desire to keep going hoping everything will fall back into place, but it won't.

As humans we are naturally sensitive, not to mention resistant, to any type of change. We want things to keep going as they always have because that is where we feel safe. I have talked about the fact I can look back and see a distinct line in my life between before and after Tim's death.

However, at the time, I didn't want to accept that it was a permanent change, so I spent months pretending as if everything was fine. I tried to force everything to be the same, but quickly found that it's not possible. Accepting that fact was one of the hardest ideas I dealt with, but it had to be done before I could move forward.

I've always had a large friend group, but I realized pretty early on, I now had much less in common with my friends who had not experienced this type of loss. I felt more distant from them as time went on as well, not because they pulled away, but because I did. So much of my life revolved around getting through my grief and keeping my business going that I didn't feel as if I had anything in common with them anymore.

> # Carrying grief is like a huge elephant in the room.

I had to accept that it's okay to change that friend group to get the support I needed. I still long for that carefree life and friend group at times, but so much has changed in my life. I'm much more aware of the struggles of those like me that I know there will always be some distance there and that's okay.

I have likened carrying that grief around those first couple of years to a huge elephant in the room. Many people don't even know it's there, but I know. It hovered over me for a long time as it does for most people. You don't step out of that shadow because you want to, and boy, I wanted to!

Your mind and your heart need that time to accept the reality of loss and then also accept the fact it will always be a part of you. That elephant shrinks over time, but it's always there and other people who have experienced loss recognize it immediately.

I prefer to think of the changes in my life as opening a whole new depth of understanding, rather than focusing on what I lost. You will have to find a perspective that allows you to accept that your old life is gone, in order to create something positive as you move on as well.

Will I ever feel in control of my life again?

A sudden death, or loss, is the ultimate realization that you have absolutely no control over life. I think we all get into a safe, secure routine of life over time, and we buy into the illusion that we are in complete control. Not only must you face the reality that we don't get to choose what happens or when, we also must face that the structure of our lives have been shaken to the core.

We are all creatures of habit, and we build the structure of our lives over time. It is so very hard to realize that the structure changed dramatically and instantly when your loved one passes. It also takes a while to accept. I still lived in the same house, went to the same job, had what I considered a somewhat regular routine, yet it wasn't the same.

Our lives as a couple had evolved to a regular work regime, working together five (sometimes six!) days per week. Enjoying golf, friends and family on Saturday and then reserving Sunday for us to cook, do things at home and enjoy being together before the work week started again. It was regular, predictable, and very enjoyable.

While my life after his death still included work, it was much more stressed, and I felt the burden of not having Tim to lean on. I no longer did those 'couple things' on the weekend and for a while didn't really go out at all. Sundays were by far the hardest in so many ways. As I've shared in previous chapters, that was 'our' time and Sunday nights was when I felt his absence the most. Those were the moments when I longed for that safe, predictable life again.

The struggle to recreate a life from the ashes of what was is so very hard and you must do it alone. You don't have that person to lean on, get advice from or enjoy their company. Those were the times I would occasionally descend into self-pity out of frustration at the constant struggle.

That is how I realized I hadn't truly and fully accepted the loss of my former life. There's nothing wrong with remembering and longing for the good times you once had. But allowing that to push you to anger and self-pity solves nothing. However, it takes time to truly accept these ideas deep in your heart, not just your head. Every time I think I'm truly 'over it' or 'past it' those feelings of frustration show themselves again.

Part of acceptance is the idea that grief goes on as long as you do. It changes and morphs over time to something much easier to deal with but it's still there. It gradually becomes the occasional wistful longing rather than plunging you into emotional anger, but it never completely leaves.

Feeling in control of your life is about not being overwhelmed. When you first lose someone you love, you absolutely will be overwhelmed. You will be overwhelmed with emotions, overwhelmed with uncertainty and overwhelmed with the details of daily life you must get through.

I can tell you that if you spend many months in denial of your feelings, as I did, that overwhelm gets worse. I didn't experience any relief from it until I accepted the idea that

I'm not perfect and neither is my grief. This realization gave me the freedom to work through the difficult emotions and create something new.

Gaining control means taking an active role in rebuilding your life. It doesn't come from trying to keep everything the same or denying the gaps that are left in your life after loss.

I understand feeling as if the world is spinning around you almost as if you are standing still in your grief. I've been there. The only way that changes is for you to take action and make positive steps forward toward a new life.

While we may perceive we have the option to stay in one place and refuse to change, we don't. Life happens whether we want it to or not and we can't stop time from relentlessly marching on. The harder you hold onto a past that doesn't exist anymore, the more out of control your life will feel.

What is going to become of me and my life now?

A very hard adjustment for us all during our grief is the idea that the future we once envisioned for ourselves, no longer exists. As couples, we all dream of our future and plan for it both financially and emotionally, some of us for literally decades. We bought a beach house years ago as an investment but with the idea we'd spend more time there when we retired. We never got to retire together at all.

I love that beach house and it has been a life saver for me in many ways because Tim and I didn't spend a lot of time there as a couple. I have been able to make it my own and it has been a wonderful refuge. However, we spent our whole married life building a business so that one day we could have a great retirement and the fact that those dreams never happened is still so very sad to me.

In addition to realizing a once dreamed of future will never be, many people who lose a spouse through death or divorce are simultaneously faced with a swift and immediate reduction in resources.

Money may, or may not, have been that big a concern before, but now it's huge. Not only did I lose my husband's income, I lost a key person in our business which had immediate consequences. Those money issues take time to fix and many people in the midst of grief also have to make some hard financial decisions.

I struggled at first like everyone does when their income is suddenly cut in half. While money problems can eventually be solved over time, the fact that you also have to reimagine a future retirement without that extra support is alarming.

There are some, especially those who have already retired, who continue to live their lives according to the dreams they had as a couple, but many more do not. When a future is imagined as a couple, but then one person is gone, it can be very sad and lonely to try to continue that dream.

Oftentimes, they realize it's easier to create a new dream that is theirs alone so they aren't imagining a future with their grief at the forefront.

Just like acceptance is a process, reimagining your future takes time. You probably won't have answers to how your life will be for months or even years down the road and that's okay. There is no timeline. Allow yourself to grow and change then make decisions based on where you are at that time rather than now.

If someone had told me how drastically my own life would change when Tim died, I would not have believed them. You may not believe me now but change after loss is inevitable and often dramatic.

One point I do want to talk about here is that some people get very defeated when they think about their future. They will have thoughts of "What's the point?" or "Why even try?"

Change after loss is inevitable and often dramatic.

I understand that thought process when you think about the future because you feel as if you have lost so much. You worked for years or decades to build a life with someone, love them and imagine a future together. Now it's all gone, and it feels as if that time was wasted. The idea that you must build all over again is a bit depressing. I get it.

All I can tell you is to keep going. Don't let those emotions of the moment get the best of you. We all have these defeatist ideas at times especially when things get hard. Those emotions are temporary and over time you will get to a point you want a positive future.

Having a supportive friend or grief professional to talk to is very important to help you shift your perspective and realize grief isn't the end. It is a huge change you must work through, but you can once again get to a good life.

The real secret is to find meaning in your life again. Helping others is one of the best ways and for me, talking to others going through the grief process has added so much to my life. I feel like maybe, after all these years, this is what my whole life has been leading up to; a way to significantly help others who are experiencing grief. You, too, will find new meaning in your life if you look for it and embrace the changes.

Will I ever feel like ME again?

This may be one of the first, and most common, questions I hear from those experiencing grief. It's one I asked too, so I know the emotions that make you feel as if you will never be 'normal' again.

In an earlier chapter I talked about the fact that when you lose someone, especially a spouse, you lose most of who you perceive yourself to be. You lose them, you lose your identity as a couple, and then you lose who you believe yourself to be. I was Mrs. Tim Domis the majority of my life. I was a wife, mother, and business partner to a well-respected man. Just because he died, doesn't mean who I perceived myself to be changed in an instant.

It took a long time for me to recreate myself as a single person. In fact, that is how the title of this book, *Table for One*, came to be. I struggled with eating alone, not because I was afraid to eat alone, but because I didn't identify myself as a single person. Single people ate alone, not me. I'd always been married. This is the part of myself I had to struggle to reimagine.

You will feel like you again, but it's a different you. It's not the person you remember yourself being when your loved one was there. You don't go 'back' to that version of you at all. Instead, you become a better, stronger, more resilient version of yourself.

I have to admit I love this version of myself so much better. Not because my life is easier, but because I'm stronger. I've proven to myself that I can come through tremendous struggle and hardship. My faith and trust in my own judgement has grown exponentially and I have recreated my life into something that brings me joy. Through my experience with Tim's death, I've also found a new calling and purpose.

I will never be the me I used to be, and I don't want that anymore. I want to continue to grow and change as a person and use the knowledge I've gained to help others.

None of us knows what we are truly capable of until faced with the hardship of grief. You will grow and change through that process just as I have. This testing by fire will produce a strong, resilient version of yourself that, while you may not be able to imagine it right now, will be someone you are very proud to be.

As a friend of mine said to me a few days after Tim died, "You will get through this, you will survive, and you will go on." I didn't believe it completely at that time, but she was right, and I share that same hope with you now.

It is not length of life but depth of life.

– Ralph Waldo Emerson

Chapter 10

Love Never Ends

*A*s you navigate a new life, you realize that grief takes up much less of your heart and mind. This doesn't mean you forget the relationship of the past, just the opposite. You get to the point you can embrace the good times from the past and not experience the stinging, raw pain of loss. Your life no longer revolves around your grief and while it is still a part of you, it is not the main emotional center of your life.

If you are reading this early on in your grief process, I realize these ideas may seem ridiculous to you right now. However, you, too, will get to this point. We all do; some sooner, some later. While the grief is completely overwhelming at first, realize it is a journey you must travel and a peaceful, satisfying life awaits you down the road.

When I was first plunged into the depths of my own emotional grief turmoil, having my friends who had previously experienced their own grief, tell there was light at the end of this horrible, long tunnel helped me hang on.

While no one, including me, can tell you what is right for you, I can share some of the things I learned as I embarked on my own life after grief. One of the most important realizations is that only you know what you need. People can offer solutions or advice or try to steer you along, but only you can make the decisions about how your life will, or will not, go.

I think of it like childbirth. Everyone has a different childbirth story, some easy and calm while others are horrific and intense. No one can compare your story to theirs and even if they try, it won't be the same.

I encourage each and every person to trust their own heart and mind when grief is so prevalent in your life you second guess everyone and everything, including yourself.

You may feel unsure and incapable of making decisions right now but give yourself some time and some grace. Trust that you are not crazy and when the emotional haze clears you will know what is right for you and your life.

Get to Know You

I would also encourage you to take the time to get to know who you are now. Allow your emotions to settle, your life to stabilize, and discover who you have now become. You will be a different person after loss and becoming comfortable with that person is critical to your long-term happiness. Do things by yourself and for yourself that you have never done and become comfortable in this new skin. Travel some, attend events, and yes, eat at that table for one!

Fully explore the newness of your changed life so you can understand yourself and your past in clear perspective. As new people enter your life, this knowledge of self will allow you to communicate better and form healthy attachments whether those are friendships or even a love interest.

For many people who have experienced the end of a long-term relationship, being single at this stage of life will be a completely new experience as it was for me. Every couple has made compromises to make their relationship work and, in those compromises, there may be things you now want to explore. This might be a hobby you always wanted to try, a novel you want to write, or simply the opportunity to spend a quiet Sunday without a football game blaring!

We choose to fit our lives into a life with another person and when that person is no longer there, who we are expands. You become the most authentic, most real version of yourself because you aren't comprising or taking someone else into consideration. There is a lot of freedom in that idea and many people really enjoy living the single life after grief simply because it may be the first time in decades, they were 100% in control of their own life and destiny.

As who we are expands, and we become more engaged by the world around us again, so many new experiences are attracted into our lives. An example in my case is attracting people who are experiencing grief into my circle of awareness. While you might think talking about grief, or listening to the grief of others, could be depressing, I find it very fulfilling. I now know what to say and what not to say for real, whereas I was only guessing before and I guessed wrong most of the time, as we all do.

Every person who has felt grief has an undeniable empathy for those who suffer loss and I think it makes us much better, more authentic people in so many ways.

The Invisibility Cloak

I have already talked in previous chapters about the fact that after a loss you often feel alone in a group of family and friends. As you are moving through those early stages of grief, it's as if you become invisible and shrink into the background as others carry on as normal. I believe that grief takes up a great deal of emotional bandwidth to the point that even normally social people become much more withdrawn. It is exhausting to try and join in when you feel so empty inside.

These feelings are completely normal. It is impossible to reengage with life when you haven't even figured out how you feel about anything yet. We all choose to sit on the sidelines for months or maybe a year or more like an animal licking its wounds. The problem comes when we start to find great comfort in that withdrawal. We carry our grief like an invisibility cloak protecting our emotions and separating ourselves from difficult situations.

I talk about this as a warning because I know several people who lost a loved one years ago and they are still in this withdrawn, disengaged stage for the most part. It is as if by choosing not to reengage they think they are protecting themselves from experiencing that kind of loss again.

I can tell you that viewpoint is not true. Life is for the living, but inevitably it comes to an end for all of us. We don't control when or how we will lose those we love whether they be partners, family, or friends.

> We don't control when or how we will lose.

As we age, the rate of these losses accelerate and while this is normal, it is still very hard for many people. They want to stop the hurt but no matter what they do it seems as if they are constantly faced with the death of another person they love or care about.

I'm in my sixties as I write this book and I can verify that this is extremely hard to deal with, so I'm not making light of it. What I do realize though, is that I'm not willing to trade the beauty and love I can still have in my life for emptiness just because loss hurts. It hurts to have no one at the end of your life, too. So while the risk of loss is always there, understand that you miss out on more than you gain by trying to go into full protection mode.

I believe at some point we long to reconnect after loss and the longer we have allowed ourselves to be seen as invisible, the more invisible we become. It takes much more effort to rejoin social events and groups of people when we now find so much comfort in being alone. However, that comfort doesn't last and if you actively choose to not engage again after loss, you will miss the best life still has to offer.

What about love?

Love enters our lives in many different ways. Sometimes through family and old friends. Sometimes through new friends or coworkers and maybe even through a new intimate partner. This may or may not be part of your new life but before you discount the idea that this is even possible, let's talk a bit more about the idea of love.

In my mind, mature love isn't solely romantic love, though it can be. As we grow through our loss, we realize that companionship, common interest, and joy for life are all equally as important, if not more so, than romantic love. In fact, these ideas are all part of how we love after loss.

I have found tremendous love and connection within the grief community while also cultivating new friendships that focus on joy and living life to the fullest. One interesting point that comes to my mind often is the fact that many of the 'friendships' I had before I lost Tim were more acquaintances, they weren't deep connections. It wasn't that I actively looked for superficial friendships, they were just there.

In contrast, I now realize that I value deep connections and authentic conversation over chit chat or talking about the weather. In fact, when I find myself in a superficial or judgmental conversation, I can feel the frustration build. I have better things to do and once you lose someone suddenly, you value time in a way you never did before. I see that quality now as a gift. I don't waste my time on people or situations that are superficial or unnecessary. I also consciously spend more time cultivating friendships that are supportive and caring because to me, that is what life is really about now.

The bottom line is that I didn't actively choose the people who were, or were not, in my life before and now I do. The suffering of grief gave me a great deal of resolve to say what I think and be who I am, no matter what anyone else thinks. I believe this may have been Tim's final gift to me and I choose to believe he'd be thrilled at how I've reengaged with my own life.

No matter where you are on your grief journey, the idea of getting back into life may be intimidating. It is normal to have conflicting emotions and uncertainty. You may feel guilt about being hopeful for your own future, but I always remember, if your loved one truly loved you, they'd want you to be happy and go on with your life so you can let that guilt go.

Right now, the unknown might be scary as you try to reimagine your life. You may long for emotional security and fear opening yourself to new people at the same time. I felt all of those emotions, sometimes all at once!

Restarting your life is an intense lesson in emotional whiplash, but it does get better as you get stronger. You will gain more clarity and confidence as time progresses and you prove to yourself that you are both strong and capable.

I would encourage you not to be too hard on yourself when you have setbacks or experience an intense wave of grief out of the blue. It happens to us all and does not take away from the progress you've made. You can have that horrible ugly cry and get right back up the next day feeling better.

Our emotions build and sometimes we need that release valve to allow us to continue. It doesn't mean we have lost control or that we are somehow not 'doing it right'. It means we are human, and we need to give ourselves a tremendous amount of latitude as we recreate our lives.

The Beauty of Self-Reflection

Reflecting on your journey as you move through grief, I have found, is extremely effective and even life changing. Its not that I didn't engage in self-reflection before Tim died, I did of course. However, it was more in the context of setting goals (professional) or New Year's resolutions (personal).

One big difference in my self-reflection then versus now, is that back before I experienced grief, I was much more concerned with what I accomplished. I set the kind of goals that included how many houses I sold, or realtors I trained in my business, and I also set goals about exercising more and traveling, in my personal life. I didn't reflect on who I wanted to be as a person or who I wanted in my life. Now, my number one concern is how happy I am and what will bring more joy to my life.

I think we all get caught in the hustle and bustle of our daily habits and rarely step back and really ask ourselves if we are happy. Are we happy in our work life? Are we happy in our relationships? Are we happy with the people we are allowing into our close friend circle? I can say I rarely thought about my life in those terms before but now, my happiness is my number one thought whenever I sit and think about how far I've come and where I'm going. My life for so long floated along and I took things as they came. I didn't feel like I was actively choosing who was in my life and who I wanted to be long term. I do now.

Much of that self-reflection comes through asking the right questions. As I stated before, as I went through my grief, I enlisted the help of a qualified therapist for a time and I still highly recommend that for those who are struggling. It convinced me I wasn't crazy, and I quickly learned to trust my own feelings and intuition.

I also enlisted the help of a professional coach. This was slightly different in that she was a person who could ask the right questions and get me thinking about who I wanted to be and how I wanted to be in the future.

Though it feels like we are being swept along by life sometimes, we do have the power to actively choose most everything about our lives. We get so overwhelmed that we forget we can say no or choose differently.

I have now taken on speaking to groups about grief and coaching others. The beauty of my suffering, I can now see, is the gift of being able to walk others through reimagining their new life.

I still encourage people to engage a grief counselor when needed, but as they grow and change many find it helpful to have a coach to ask the right questions and guide them forward to true happiness.

The biggest value to me was having a person who is not emotionally connected to Tim, my family, or my business. I felt that gave me an objective insight from a third party that I really didn't have in my life at the time and that is what I now offer for others.

We all are impacted and changed forever by our experiences and grief is one of the most life changing. But that doesn't mean those changes are necessarily bad. I think they can be very educational and profound as you learn more about yourself and what you are really capable of. As you gain strength, you lose much of the fear or hesitancy to try new things or engage with new people.

This expands your world and your experiences. While life after grief will never be the same, it can be as good or better, YOU can be as good or better. There is something so fulfilling, after having felt completely broken for so long, to now be able to say I'm happy and very fulfilled once again.

There is no 'one way' to happiness but by embracing your own journey through the dark horrible turmoil of grief you can find happiness again. I encourage you to gather all your strength and face the obstacles with as much courage as possible knowing there will be times you struggle. There will be times you fail. There will be times you triumph.

The journey through grief will shape you anew both mentally and emotionally. You will be more prepared for the rest of your life and when grief happens in your life again, you will understand yourself and your grief so much better.

There are so many people I talk to who have lost more than one spouse throughout their lives. It doesn't seem to matter how long they were together or how they lived their lives; the grief is still different.

I have one friend who was married more than 25 years to her high school sweetheart. When he died, her grief was intense, but she was able to move on and create a great life.

She remarried and her second husband died 8 years after they married. This time her grief was debilitating. In talking with her and thinking about the reasons she experienced this grief so differently, the conclusion we both came to was they were completely different people. Her husbands were clearly different, but she was also a different person in each relationship.

I share this only to let you know you will never experience this specific kind of grief again. Each grief is unique to the relationship you had with that person, and the person you were when you lost them.

This idea is important because grief isn't a lesson we learn once, it is an experience that changes us as we change with it. I personally find some comfort in that. I know that when, not if, I encounter grief again I will be more prepared not to prevent the emotions, but to embrace them and allow myself to start the healing process. That doesn't mean it will be easier, I'll just be more knowledgeable.

The various facets of who we are, and who we will be, are shaped and shifted over time and through these intense emotional experiences. I choose to find the positive after these terrible events even if it takes some time to understand them.

My greatest hope through this book is that you understand that the path forward through grief is not easy, but it is one of hope. There is life after grief. Your life can, and will, have a positive outcome if you choose for it to.

While none of that personal growth is easy or fast, it is worthwhile as you gain a new understanding of who you are and how you want to live.

I encourage you to continue your journey of growth and happiness knowing that these dark days will fade and one day, you will once again walk in the sun.

Note from the Author

Thank you so much for reading my story of hope after loss. I would like to ask you to please go to Amazon.com, or your favorite book review site, and leave a review of this book!

Thank You,

Linda C. Domis

About the Author

Linda C. Domis experienced every emotion imaginable in her own journey through grief. After suddenly losing her husband and business partner of 40+ years, she wished desperately for some kind of guide for people like her, that was real and useful.

She wrote *Table for One* to be that guide for others. While no one is immune from the emotional trauma of death, knowing what to expect in real, relatable terms can give hope that there is a good and fulfilling life after loss.

CPSIA information can be obtained
at www.ICGtesting.com
Printed in the USA
LVHW041237291022
731798LV00008B/777